Praise for Casey Schwartz's

ATTENTION
A Personal History of Finding Focus (or Trying To)

"The culmination of a quest to understand attention, especially in the context of digital addiction and burnout. . . . Its three-quarter-inch binding betrays its breadth. . . . Schwartz deploys history as a balm for anxious readers."
—*Vanity Fair*

"Casey Schwartz is a formidable reporter, a rigorous researcher, and a true artist of prose. She makes complicated information easily understood and elevates seemingly simple observations to a richer plane of meaning. More than that, though (and this is the toughest job in the business), she is an honest broker when it comes to telling her own story."
—Meghan Daum, author of *The Problem with Everything: My Journey Through the New Culture Wars*

"A personal and professional study of the struggle with attention in an age of distraction. . . . Unfailingly honest. . . . By personalizing her account, and her journey, [Schwartz] enhances the book's potency without diluting its authority. . . . Being attentive is an acquired skill. Schwartz helps us think deeply and clearly about what it offers us."
—*Kirkus Reviews* (starred review)

"Essential. . . . *Attention* asks two simple questions: 'Why are we so susceptible to all the escape routes our technologies offer us in the first place?' and 'What are we fleeing?'"

—*Bitch Media*

"Schwartz's book brims with ideas. . . . Schwartz is unusually self-aware, though she may not always think so. She is honest about her own vulnerabilities and self-doubt. . . . By personalizing her account . . . she makes it a vivid, memorable thing, not simply instructive."

—*The Post and Courier* (Charleston, SC)

"An antidote to the countless manuals devoted to attention-hacking and technology detox, the tired denouncements of our iPhone dependence. . . . It is consistently interesting and beautifully written." —*New Statesman*

"An insightful hybrid of memoir and academic study. . . . Thought-provoking. . . . This is a rich inquiry into what it means to pay (and maintain) attention in a world increasingly permeated with distraction and interference."

—*Publishers Weekly*

"With fascinating research and illuminating interviews, this is ruminative, provocative, and discussion-worthy." —*Booklist*

Casey Schwartz

ATTENTION

A Personal History of Finding Focus (or Trying To)

Casey Schwartz is the author of *In the Mind Fields*. She contributes regularly to *The New York Times* and lives in New York City.

www.caseyschwartz.com

Also by Casey Schwartz

In the Mind Fields:
Exploring the New Science of Neuropsychoanalysis

ATTENTION

A Personal History of Finding Focus (or Trying To)

ATTENTION

A Personal History of Finding Focus (or Trying To)

Casey Schwartz

Vintage Books
A Division of Penguin Random House LLC
New York

FIRST VINTAGE BOOKS EDITION, SEPTEMBER 2021

Copyright © 2020, 2021 by Casey Schwartz

All rights reserved. Published in the United States by Vintage Books,
a division of Penguin Random House LLC, New York, and distributed
in Canada by Penguin Random House Canada Limited, Toronto. Published
in hardcover in the United States by Pantheon Books, a division of
Penguin Random House LLC, New York, in 2020.

Vintage and colophon are registered trademarks of
Penguin Random House LLC.

This is a work of nonfiction, but the names of certain individuals,
as well as identifying descriptive details concerning them,
have been changed to protect their privacy.

Excerpt of "Praying" from *Thirst* by Mary Oliver, published in the United States
by Beacon Press, Boston, Massachusetts, in 2006. Copyright © 2006 by Mary
Oliver. Reprinted by permission of the Charlotte Sheedy Literary Agency, Inc.

The Library of Congress has cataloged the Pantheon edition as follows:
Name: Schwartz, Casey, author.
Title: Attention : a love story /
Casey Schwartz.
Description: First edition. | New York : Pantheon Books, 2020.
Identifiers: LCCN 2019027783 (print) | LCCN 2019027784 (ebook)
Subjects: LCSH: Schwartz, Casey. | Attention. | Attention-deficit hyperactivity
disorder. | Distraction (Psychology). | Information technology—Social aspects.
Classification: LCC BF321 .S337 2020 (print) | LCC BF321 (ebook) |
DDC 153.7/33—dc23
LC record available at https://lccn.loc.gov/2019027783
LC ebook record available at https://lccn.loc.gov/2019027784

Vintage Books Trade Paperback ISBN: 978-0-525-43598-3
eBook ISBN: 978-1-5247-4711-4

Author photograph © Beowulf Sheehan
Book design by Anna B. Knighton

www.vintagebooks.com

146119709

For J.K. and, as always, M.B.

Part I

SEDUCTION

This story begins with the Adderall. I am referring to the pills that entered my life, as they did so many lives, when I was eighteen years old and stayed lodged there until I was thirty. These pills seemed to offer me pure, distilled attention any time I needed it, to compensate for whatever I imagined my deficiencies in that department to be.

And, like any love story, I remember everything about the moment it began. In 2000, I was a freshman at Brown University. One night, still in our first term, I'd come to complain to a friend about the situation in which I found myself: an essay due the following afternoon on a book I had yet to read. All around us, her clothes were strewn messily on her dorm room floor. "Do you want an Adderall?" she asked. "I can't stand them. They make me want to stay up all night doing cartwheels in the hall." Could there be a more enticing description? From a ball of tin-foil, she pulled out a single pill, the deep bright blue of a cartoon sky. My hand shot out to receive it. I had come there merely to vent, but I left with my first Adderall—a medication prescribed for attention deficit hyperactivity disorder, or ADHD, a condition I knew nothing about, except for some vague awareness of classmates in high school who had needed extra time when taking their exams. At the time my friend unfurled her tinfoil ball, Adderall had been on the market roughly four years, but it was brand-new to me.

An hour later, I was in the basement of the Rock, our nickname for the library, hunkered down in the Absolute Quiet Room, in a state of ecstasy. The world fell away; it was only me, locked in the passionate embrace of the book in front of me, and the thoughts I was having about it, which tumbled out of nowhere and built into what seemed a pile of riches. When dawn came to Providence, I was hunched over in the grubby lounge of my dormitory, typing my last fevered perceptions, barely aware that outside the window, the sky was turning pink. I was alone in my secret new world, and that aloneness was part of the great intoxication. I needed for nothing and no one.

I didn't know it then, but it was actually in Providence, nearly seventy years before, that Benzedrine, an amphetamine-based precursor to Adderall, had been given one of its first test runs. In 1937, at the Emma Pendleton Bradley Home for disturbed and difficult children, Dr. Charles Bradley performed the first of two experiments to test the effects of Benzedrine on children. The pills were created as decongestants but were also known to boost moods in adults. Dr. Bradley was surprised by the results: the kids calmed down, became less rowdy and raucous, and seemed to gobble up their school lessons with relish. They became, in other words, rapturously, singularly, *focused*.

Like those difficult children before me, I would experience this same sensation again and again over the next four years, whenever I could get my hands on Adderall, which was frequently but not, I felt, frequently enough. There were ways of getting more, each of them shrouded in a thick ethical dinginess. For instance: The campus black market, where the ADHD kids sold off their prescriptions at exorbitant markups. The heiress whose pills I swiped while attending her numerous parties. Later, the barter system, wherein I helped with other people's essays in exchange for their meds.

Quickly, my Adderall hours became the most precious hours of my life, far too precious for the Absolute Quiet Room. I now needed to locate the most remote desk in the darkest, most neglected corner of the upper-level stacks, tucked farthest away from the humming campus life outside. That life no longer interested me. Instead, what mattered, what compelled, were the hours I spent in isolation, poring over, for instance, Immanuel Kant's thoughts on "the sublime." I read and reread the lines. The text was difficult, but my attention was now unflagging, bionic. The single greatest impediment to comprehension had been removed. The Kantian enigma clicked into place.

It was fitting: *this* was sublime, these afternoons I spent in untrammeled focus, absorbing the complicated ideas in the books in front of me, mastering them, penetrating every inch of their surface with my razor-like comprehension, making them a part of myself. Or rather, of what I now thought of as my self, which is to say, the steely, undistractible person whom I vastly preferred to the lazier, glitchier person I secretly knew my actual self to be, the one who was subject to fits of lassitude and a tendency to eat too many Swedish Fish.

I don't think that in the years before I took that first blue pill, I had consciously doubted my own ability to focus. But once I tried Adderall, I couldn't forget what it promised me: a quality of attention that I now idolized and craved. It was attention weaponized, slashing through procrastination and self-doubt, returning me to a place that felt almost like childhood, with its unclouded pleasures of rapt hours, lost in books and imagination. Childhood, but with a jittery amphetamine edge.

Another thing: Adderall wiped away the question of willpower. I could study all night, then run ten miles, then breeze that week's *New Yorker,* all without pausing to consider whether I might prefer to lie around, or go to the movies. It was fantastic. I lost weight. That was nice too. Deeper into the Adderall years, I started to snap at friends, abruptly accessing huge depths of fury I wouldn't have thought I possessed. When a roommate went home one weekend and forgot to turn off her alarm clock so that it beeped behind her locked door for forty-eight hours, I entirely lost control, calling her in New York to berate her. My anger, unhinged as it was, felt out of proportion to the crime. God knows how long it had been since I had slept more than five hours. Why bother?

As much as I loved Adderall, which I did, from the earliest moments I also knew that, ultimately, nothing good could come of our entanglement. By senior year of college, my schoolwork had grown more, not less, unmanageable. I'd been accepted to a program called the Capstone, which I'd aspired to since I'd first arrived on campus. Instead of writing the usual thesis required for an honors degree, I would write a novella-length fiction manuscript, working with a faculty advisor in weekly editorial sessions. I was assigned to a new member of the creative writing faculty, one who had arrived on campus in a cloud of intrigue, having parted ways with the Mormon Church due to the heretical content of his novels. Or so I'd heard. He and I never really advanced beyond an awkward politeness. Our arrangement, such as it was, usually involved my telling him I was too far behind to profit from our slotted editorial meetings. And so, week after week, we would cancel.

As the first semester neared an end, I was behind on the manuscript, and behind on all my other schoolwork as well. My droll, aristocratic Russian history professor granted me an extension on the final term paper. One Friday evening, well into December, when the idyllic New England campus had already begun to empty out for the winter holiday, I was alone at the Sciences Library—the one that stayed open the latest—squinting down at my notes on the Russian intelligentsia. Outside, it was blizzarding. Inside, the fluorescent lights beat down on the empty basement-level room. I felt dizzy and strange. It had been a particularly chemical week; several days had passed since I'd slept more than a handful of hours, taking more and more pills to compensate. When I looked up from the page, the bright room seemed to dilate around me, as if I weren't really there, but rather stuck in some strange mirage. I seized with panic—what was happening? I tried to breathe, to snap myself back into reality. Shakily, I stood and made my way toward the phone. I dialed my friend Dave in his dorm room. "I'm having some kind of problem at the SciLi," I told him. My own voice sounded like it belonged to someone else.

Soon, I was in an ambulance, being taken through the snowstorm to the nearest hospital. The volunteer EMT was a Brown student whom I'd met once or twice. He held my hand the whole way. "Am I going to die?" I kept asking him. Dave and I sat for hours in the emergency room, until I was ushered behind a curtain and a skeptical-looking doctor came in to see me. I wasn't used to being looked at the way he was looking at me, which is to say, like I was insane, an unstable force he needed to contain. By then I was feeling better, no longer so sure I was dying, and as I lay down on the examination table, I joked to him: "I will recline, like the Romans!" His expression remained unamused. His diagnosis: "Anxiety, amphetamine induced." I had had my first panic attack, an uncommon but by no means unknown reaction to taking too much Adderall. When I left the hospital, I left behind the canister of blue pills that I had painstakingly scrounged together. I still remember the sight of it sitting next to the bed.

I'd had a drug overdose, which seemed like the kind of thing one told one's parents about. That particular week, my mother, a magazine journalist, was in Europe, deep into the reporting of her latest piece. I didn't want to call her to say that I had OD'ed on Adderall and gone to the hospital, because she might feel she had to come home and, after all, I was *fine*. So instead I called my father, whose own parenting style was much less traditional. My parents were long divorced and it was possible, with my father, especially, to keep secrets. On the phone, I told him what had happened. I told him that in the emergency room, it had shocked me to be looked at as if I were nuts. He interrupted me, his voice uncharacteristically stern. "Well, in point of fact, you *were* nuts. You were *nuts* to take that number of pills." He also mentioned, while we were on the subject, that he had felt, for the last two years, more and more, that I had become "unavailable" and "removed." I promised him I would stop the Adderall. And in that moment, I meant it. A few days later, I drew incompletes in all my classes and came home to New York, where I spent the long winter break at the Forty-Second Street public library, lethargically soldiering through the essays I hadn't been able to cope with while taking amphetamines.

I suppose this is the place to mention that in New York, I had grown up in a community of writers and journalists, a world that prized curiosity and concentration. One constant soundtrack of my childhood was my mother, playing tapes: the recordings of interviews she'd done, the building blocks of the long articles she would write. From her office, I could hear endless hours of faceless voices as she sat there—at her typewriter, and then at her computer—constructing meaning, narrative, a way to understand what was being revealed. The tapes would unspool, guided by my mother's inexhaustible questions, her subjects' obliging answers. Her native Texas accent has long since been buried beneath her decades in New York, but the Texas in her lives on: she is the ultimate question asker, as much in everyday conversation as in her life as a journalist. In fact, for her, and now, unavoidably, for me, asking questions has always been the very definition of good manners: to show curiosity about another human being. And mean it.

My father too was a writer, when he wasn't on the radio, playing the Great American Songbook, Sinatra and Ella and Billie Holiday, and all the rest of the voices from that musically charmed era. He would tell me about his weeks in the California desert, where he disappeared to get his four books written, the routine of waking up at dawn, making coffee, and then just sitting there.

Sitting there: that was key, apparently. I would have to master that ability, then, because for as long as I remembered, I had known that I had wanted to write. Through my childhood, my father would press his favorite authors on me, his every tone and gesture conveying their sacred importance: Philip Roth, J. D. Salinger, Elizabeth Hardwick, Renata Adler. These writers and their books were what we often talked about in our time together, which was limited because of the divorce. My father would tell me in his supercharged way: "Writing is one of the hardest jobs. I believe it's what you're going to do." We were on a swing set in Carl Schurz Park, overlooking the East River, the first time I remember him saying that to me. I was five or six years old.

Back on campus after the winter holiday, I was soon also back on the old chemical regimen. I was locked again into the familiar pattern, the blissful intensity and isolation, followed by days of slow-motion comedown, when I would laze around for hours, gobbling ice cream straight from the carton, desperate for the sugar rush, barely able to muster the energy to take a shower.

My main concern now was my Capstone manuscript. I was by then so in thrall to Adderall that I was convinced I couldn't sustain the creative impulse without it, that my attention would wander to trivial pursuits if I didn't supercharge it with prescription speed. That was what so many writers had done before me, wasn't it? Kerouac and the rest of the Beats, Graham Greene, Susan Sontag, W. H. Auden. I was simply following in the grand tradition of so many transatlantic geniuses. This was what I told myself.

My writing process consisted of jagged, sleepless nights, humorless stretches of time in which I would lock myself away from my noisy roommates to conjure the amphetamine intensity that I mistook for real work. By the spring, I was so far behind on the manuscript that, in desperation, I spent the spring vacation—my last one in college—not with my friends or family, but alone in a cheap hotel room in Miami. I stayed up for days on too much Adderall, typing frantically in the red glow that came in from the garish lights of South Beach. When I felt stuck, I would walk up and down the beach in a furious state, castigating myself, at a remove from every human being around me. An irony: the manuscript I was writing was about a young man struggling with addiction, but I never thought to connect it to my own, or even to acknowledge that I had one. In the end, I finished it, but I felt a sense of deep shame attached to the manuscript, as if the pages themselves were contaminated. I turned it over to my ex-Mormon authority figure. Though his comments were generous, I did not look at it again for more than a decade.

It took me exactly one year from the time of college graduation to come to the decision that would, to a great extent, shape the next phase of my life. It hit me like a revelation: it might be possible to declare my independence from the various ADHD kids who sold me their prescription pills and get a prescription all my own. The idea came as I walked among the palm trees on the campus of UCLA. By then, I was living in Los Angeles, working as a private tutor for high school kids (many of whom were themselves on Adderall) and taking summer school classes in psychology and neuroscience, in order to be able to apply for graduate school. I was going to train in psychology, a route that seemed infinitely more realistic than trying to make a career as a writer, I had decided. Like many twentysomethings, my decisions were informed by panic and haste, but, as well, by whatever short-lived supply of the pills I happened to be in possession of.

I was now surrounded—or had surrounded myself—by others caught in the Adderall web. Two of my closest friends that year were both brimming with ambition and both the children of unusually accomplished parents. Together, we traversed the city in a state of perpetual, hyped-up intensity, exchanging confidences that later we would not recall. Adderall was the currency of our friendship; when one of us ran short of pills, another would cover the deficit. Driving through Los Angeles in a sun-drenched trance, weaving in and out of traffic, it was all too easy to lose track of exactly how many pills one had swallowed that day.

More than ten years later, I would sit in a café in Manhattan with one of those friends and listen as she told me that, after years of secrecy and shady behavior, disappearing into silence for increasingly long intervals, failing to show up for dinners and parties and all the occasions that keep friendships glued together, she had now, finally, managed to get off the pills. But not before she quit her prestigious job and moved out of the city, and in with her much older lover, who had a zero-tolerance policy about drug use. "I had to make it life or death to get off the Adderall," my friend told me. "Actually, I think it might really have been life or death."

But that was in our wised-up thirties. At twenty-two, when it occurred to me that I might be able to get my own prescription, I went to the nearest campus computer and Googled "cognitive behavioral psychiatrist," Los Angeles. I knew enough about psychology by then to know I should avoid the psychoanalysts who would want to go deep, and talk to me for weeks or maybe months about why I felt I needed chemical enhancement. No, I couldn't turn to them: I needed a therapist with an MD, a focus on concrete "results." And one whose office was as nearby as possible. The very next day, I was sitting in exactly the kind of office I had envisioned, an impersonal room with black leather furniture, describing to the attractive olive-skinned figure in the chair opposite me how I had always had to develop elaborate compensatory strategies for getting through my schoolwork, how staying with any one thing was a challenge for me, how I was best at jobs that required elaborate multitasking, like waitressing. Untrue, all of it. I was a focused student and a terrible waitress. And yet, these were the answers that I had discovered from the briefest online research were characteristic of the ADHD diagnostic criteria. These were the answers they were looking for in order to pick up their pens and write down "Adderall, 20 mg, once a day." So these were the answers I gave.

A brief word about ADHD, four letters that have crept into American life, taking up position as if they've always been there. Prior to ADHD there was ADD, for attention deficit disorder, a diagnosis that first appeared in the 1980 edition of the *DSM,* the handbook of American psychiatry. Yet this was only its latest incarnation. Before ADHD and before ADD, there was the much less palatable-sounding "minimal brain dysfunction" that had been in use for decades. It was a label that was admittedly vague. As Alan Schwarz writes in his potent book on the subject, *ADHD Nation:* "If the syndrome were *minimal,* why use such serious medications to treat it? If it involved the *brain,* why didn't anything show up on cerebral scans? And what constituted *dysfunction,* anyway? What was wrong with these kids medically?"

According to Schwarz, one of the earliest to put a name to it was the Scottish doctor Sir Alexander Crichton. Working in the final decades of the eighteenth century at London's Westminster Hospital, Crichton depicted the overly distractible as an official type warranting inclusion in a textbook of medical conditions. He gave an entire chapter to the issue of "Attention and its diseases" in his compendious two-volume work *An Inquiry into the Nature and Origin of Mental Derangement,* writing that "[i]n this disease of attention, if it can with propriety be called so, every impression seems to agitate the person, and gives him or her an unnatural degree of mental restlessness. People walking up and down the room, a slight noise, in the same, the mowing, the shutting a door suddenly, a slight excess of heat or of cold, too much light or too little light, all destroy constant attention in such [patients]." (If Crichton knew that I had just spent the last hour fuming over a man playing the guitar outside my apartment building, would he diagnose my attention as diseased? I sense he might.)

But attention and its discontents remained a question that no physician was able to sufficiently categorize until, Schwarz argues, the psychologist Virginia Douglas presented a paper to the Canadian Psychological Association in 1971, describing her work with hyperactive children. Douglas's innovation was to put forward a new way of formulating the deficit in these particular cases: attention. Attention was at the heart of the vague, swirling constellation of problem behavior that doctors had not quite managed to pin down. Douglas's observation seemed to crystallize the central pathology with these cases, around which every other symptom could now be arrayed. What was wrong, starting in 1971, was that these children could not pay attention.

In the 1990s, an estimated 3 to 5 percent of American children were believed to have disordered attention, according to the Centers for Disease Control and Prevention; by 2013, that figure was 11 percent. And, of course, the increase in diagnoses has been followed by an increase in pharmaceutical prescriptions. In 1990, six hundred thousand children were on stimulants, usually Ritalin, an older medication that often had to be taken multiple times a day. By 2013, 3.5 million children were on stimulants, and in many cases, the Ritalin had been replaced by Adderall, officially brought to market in 1996 as the new, upgraded choice for ADHD: more effective, longer lasting. Adderall's very name reflects its makers' hopes for an expanding customer base: "ADD for all" is the phrase that inspired it,

Alan Schwarz reports. By the time I arrived at college in 2000, four years after Adderall hit the market, nearly five million prescriptions had been written. By 2005, it was just under nine million. Sales of ADHD medication totaled more than $2 billion that year.

And by 2005, I had officially joined this attention economy. I stood on San Vicente Boulevard in the bright California sun, my prescription slip in hand. That single doctor's assessment, granted in less than an hour, would follow me all over the world: through the rest of my time in Los Angeles, then off to London for graduate school with the help of Federal Express, then to New Haven, where I would pick it up once a month at the Yale Health Clinic, then back to New York, where the GP I found through my insurance plan would have no problem prescribing this medication, based only on my saying that it had previously been prescribed to me, that I'd been taking it for years. But in that first moment, out on San Vicente Boulevard, I was in a strange mood, one I wouldn't have predicted. Walking toward the nearest pharmacy to have my first prescription filled, I felt suddenly, entirely, alone.

Any basic neuroscience textbook will explain how Adderall works in the brain—and why it's so hard to break the habit. For years, the predominant explanation of addiction has revolved around the neurotransmitter dopamine. Amphetamines unleash dopamine along with norepinephrine; they rush through the brain's synapses and increase levels of arousal, attention, vigilance, and motivation. Dopamine, in fact, tends to feature in every experience that feels especially great, be it having sex or eating chocolate cake. It's for this reason that dopamine is so heavily implicated in current models of addiction. As a person begins to overuse a substance, the brain—which craves homeostasis and fights for it—tries to compensate for all the extra dopamine by stripping out its own dopamine receptors. With the reduction of dopamine receptors, the person needs more and more of her favored substance to produce the euphoria it once offered her. The vanishing dopamine receptors also help explain the agony of withdrawal: without that favored substance, a person is left with a brain whose capacity to experience reward is well below its natural levels. It is an open question whether every brain returns to its original settings once off the drug.

"Adderall is not meaningfully different from methamphetamine," says Carl Hart, a professor of psychology and psychiatry at Columbia University, in between bites of a baked sweet potato. I have come to see him in the spring of 2016, now intent on telling the story of my years on Adderall, and my search for attention in its aftermath. Hart studies psychoactive drug effects in humans; he is also a forceful advocate in the struggle to revise how we think about drug addiction. Hart doesn't look like your typical academic, with his Hollywood-caliber handsomeness and charisma, his long dreadlocks tied back in a ponytail. We sit together in his office at Columbia, on Manhattan's Upper West Side. When I arrive, he is guzzling green juice from a glass jar, wearing a T-shirt that depicts, in bright blue outline, an amphetamine compound. He points to his shirt to demonstrate how easy it would be to convert amphetamine to methamphetamine. "You just add one methyl group," he tells me. "The drugs produce the same effects. They are essentially the same drug."

In Hart's view, the "dopamine hypothesis" of drug addiction is overly simplistic. The problem with how most of us think about drug abuse, he says, is in our failure to look past the substance itself to the larger human context around it. In fact, given our context, "Adderall is a smart choice. In our driven society, it's a logical choice." Adderall seems, on the surface of things, to fit so well with how life is, speed for the sped-up Internet age. Indeed, as I look back on it, it does not escape me that just as Adderall was surging onto the market in the 1990s, so was the World Wide Web, that the two have ascended in American life in perfect lockstep, like a disease and a cure, made for each other.

2

Have you ever been to Enfield? I had never even heard of it until I moved from Los Angeles to London for graduate school in the fall of 2006. One afternoon, soon after I got there, I received a notification that a package whose arrival I had been anticipating for days had been bogged down in customs and was currently in limbo in a FedEx warehouse in Enfield, an unremarkable London suburb. I was outside my flat within minutes of receiving this news and on the train to Enfield within the hour, staring through the window at the gray sky. The package in question, sent from LA, contained my monthly supply of Adderall.

I had come to London to study psychoanalysis at the Anna Freud Centre—a clinic for children founded in 1952 by Freud's youngest daughter, Anna. It was now a training program for future psychoanalysts, housed in a narrow redbrick town house in North London, across the street from where the Freuds themselves had lived after fleeing Vienna in 1938. Arriving in

Hampstead, I found myself at the very epicenter of an old-fashioned universe where, I often felt, time had stood still and the human mind, in all its mysteriousness, was still dissected with wonder and reverence.

I began to explore my new city, walking along the high streets that sloped up to Hampstead Heath and marveling at the subtle manifestations of Englishness all around me, a code I was just beginning to learn. There was a shift in pace, I noticed, room for slowness, at least as compared with New York. Yet I had brought my New York–paced drug with me, and I doused myself with it in the usual way. On one of those early London days, as dusk settled over the city, a wave of sadness flooded me with such an acute intensity that my eyes filled with tears. I hurried my pace through the streets of Primrose Hill, as if to outrun the gloom. I was here, in this magical new city, on a perfect fall evening in my early twenties, but I was also stuck, at a remove, unable to register with full force my new circumstances. It was as though the Adderall had coated my nerve endings in wax, blunting and blurring my experience of the world. The sadness I felt that evening was not uncommon, but it has stayed in my mind more vividly than its many counterpart occasions. It was, I understand now, a premonition of all the beauty I was going to miss as long as I stayed on this drug.

I came back to New York for the Christmas holiday and promptly broke my right foot in an unfortunate Vespa incident. In the weeks that followed, I lay on my childhood bed, contemplating the black plastic boot propped up on the pillows. I downed Adderall to fill the horizontal days, then Vicodin to take the edge off. I was trapped, I knew, powerless to free myself now. My mother came and lay down next to me. She sensed some deeper problem, something beyond the usual hell of being twenty-four. But she didn't know what it was. For once in her career as an investigative journalist, she didn't have the full story.

It wasn't until the following year, now back in the United States for the second half of graduate school, studying neuroscience at Yale, that I found myself in a psychiatrist's office, sobbing to him that my life was no longer my own. Going to see this man represented my first concerted effort to get off the Adderall. I was lucky to find myself in the presence of someone so kind and calm, an addiction specialist from Belgrade, who observed my distress with sympathy and prescribed me Wellbutrin, an antidepressant with a slightly speedy quality that could cushion the blow of withdrawal and make it less painful to get off the Adderall. His theory was sound, but soon enough, I was simply taking both medications together.

A few months later, now finished with graduate school, I sat down with my Adderall to hammer out a book proposal. Psychology wasn't the field I wanted to enter, but rather, I'd try to write about it: psychoanalysis and neuroscience, the clash of the old and the new. When I look back on that twenty-six-year-old now, I try to see her the way her friends and family saw her: functioning if panicky, done with graduate school and beginning to write her first book. From the outside, it was hardly an alarming portrait. The inside was another story.

As I began to work on the book, buried in reams of neuroscience literature, I was perfectly positioned to read the many details now surfacing about the effects of amphetamines on the brain and, by extension, on inner life. One finding struck me as particularly chilling: Jaak Panksepp, a neuroscientist who studied emotional systems in animals, found that stimulants significantly suppress signs of play and playfulness in rats. I identified completely with those slavish rats: I thought of myself at my desk, my mind riveted with maniacal intensity to the writing effort before me, with so little room left for serendipity. Another finding came from Kent Berridge's lab at the University of Michigan, where researchers showed that, in neurological terms, "liking" something was not the same thing as "wanting" it. Rather, these two sensations emanate from two different places in the brain, demonstrating that there is a physical basis for what so many people who have struggled with addiction already know: our brains can send us the signal that we need something, even when we have come to despise it.

These findings, and others, took on a greater salience for me as the months went by. Bogged down in the effort to write my book, I had the sense I'd become imprisoned in a joyless little cave of concentration, my world narrowed down to the tiniest groove. I clearly saw the strangeness of my situation: I spent my days immersed in reams of research coming out of the brain world, while constantly, privately tinkering with my own brain chemistry, pushing it this way and that, hypervigilant to each and every dip in energy, terrified of torpor, as if I couldn't afford to lose a single minute to the body's natural ebbs and flows. I wanted my own cycle, my own rhythm: I wanted to be always on, always up, always ready.

The boyfriend I lived with during this time, David, was horrified by the place of Adderall in our relationship. Extremely sensitive, he could identify whether or not I'd taken a pill simply by viewing my face: he once spotted the presence of Adderall in my expression from all the way down the block. Despairing, he came home from a trip and showed me a collection of addiction literature he'd bought at the airport to try to cope with our situation, including a book called *Willpower's Not Enough*. This book in particular, he told me, had saved our relationship. For the moment.

I felt increasingly trapped by David, by his presence in my little apartment on Ninth Street, his searing perceptions and judgments. Whenever I could, I left town, taking solo trips to a cousin's beach house in the middle of winter to "work on my book." That's where I was when, over the phone, David and I decided to break up. Less than a year before, he had moved to New York from Los Angeles to live with me. Years later, now a dear friend, he would tell me that during that phone call, when he floated the idea of splitting up, I had let out an audible sigh of relief. Of course: I could now take my Adderall in peace.

Well, not peace exactly. I still had my own awareness of how toxic this drug was to spoil the fun. Around this time, a journalist friend, much more experienced, told me that, when she'd first been made a staff writer at a prestigious magazine, she had used cocaine—similar to Adderall in chemical effect—to begin every assignment, trying to overcome the terror and self-doubt that seemed to spring up from the blank page. Once every few weeks, she would go downtown and refresh her supply from a voluble, overweight Greek man. One day, when she arrived at his apartment, he turned to her abruptly. "This is *terrible* drug for writers," he said. "It destroys relationship with the past."

I did not show it, but I was deeply shaken by her story. I knew exactly what that Greek man meant. High on uppers—be it cocaine or Adderall—you're not likely to access the depths, to bring to bear every inch of experience, sensibility, and emotion that all good writing requires. And yet, I continued. I somehow needed to enter that state of hyperreality—heart rate elevated, peripheral vision blurred, palms damp, mind strictly singular—in order to type sentences onto my computer screen. Whether or not they were the right sentences—truthful, full of true feeling—was a different concern, one that I worried about constantly. It was the question that plagued me when I lay awake at three in the morning, or even when I didn't. Many nights I had the same dream: I was pregnant, but had unwittingly been taking drugs the whole time; it was too late now, and the baby would be born with horrible deformities. I told myself that by taking the Adderall, I was exerting total control over my own fallible self, but in truth it was the opposite: the Adderall made my life unpredictable, blowing black storm systems across my mental horizon with no warning at all.

As I struggled to make headway with my book, I had a day job as a reporter for a news website. Every morning I ate an egg sandwich, chased it down with an Adderall, and, deliciously, dangerously jittery, headed out to the office, a modern glass boat of a building overlooking the Hudson. What was required of me there was the constant filing of short, catchy pieces: to be quick and glib, and move on. The work seemed to be the rhythm most suited to an Adderall-head like me—and the kind of writing most at odds with the effort to think slowly and carefully, at book length, the way I had observed both my parents working, all through my childhood. In the new world of the Internet, the very goal of slow and careful thinking came to feel more and more anachronistic with each passing week.

The warm embrace of Adderall on college campuses and beyond soon produced a success story within the scientific community. In 2008, the journal *Nature* published a commentary, which quickly made headlines, written by a group of prestigious neuroscientists, neurologists, and neuro-ethicists. Their statement was a kind of declaration: no longer did it make sense to regard cognitive enhancement medication as philosophically questionable. Instead, this commentary suggested, the pills were a fact of modern life and should be understood in the same terms as eating kale, taking vitamins, and getting on the treadmill, just another weapon in the armament of bourgeois ambition. Referring to Ritalin and Adderall, they wrote:

> The drugs just reviewed, along with newer technologies such as brain stimulation and prosthetic brain chips, should be viewed in the same general category as education, good health habits, and information technology—ways that our uniquely innovative species tries to improve itself . . . Cognitive enhancement has much to offer individuals and society, and a proper societal response will involve making enhancements available while managing their risks.

The commentary made clear that the authors' equanimity, if not downright enthusiasm, toward drugs like Adderall—or, at least, the *idea* of drugs like Adderall—was firm, despite a swarm of unanswered questions, questions that the authors themselves delineated. These included, but were not limited to: "What are the risks of dependence when used for cognitive enhancement? What special risks arise with the enhancement of children's cognition? How big are the effects of currently available enhancers? Do they change 'cognitive style' as well as increasing how quickly and accurately we think? And given that most research so far has focused on simple laboratory tasks, how do they affect cognition in the real world?"

These were not minor questions. Rather, they concerned the very nature of how Adderall affects the brain and the mind. A decade later, they are still largely unresolved.

Yet, in 2016, when I spoke to Martha Farah, a cognitive neuroscientist at the University of Pennsylvania and one of the authors of the 2008 commentary in *Nature,* she struck a different note. What was now clear to Farah, in large part because of her own lab's research, was that Adderall, billed as a cognitive enhancing medication and embraced by the neuro-intelligentsia as such, might not actually work. At least, not as it is commonly understood to work.

Since 2008, Farah and others have been looking more carefully at whether people's performances in cognitively challenging situations actually do improve on Adderall. Farah has tested Adderall's effect on a host of standardized tasks, from the "go/no-go task," which examines how well participants are able to restrain themselves from pushing a button in response to the wrong targets, to tasks that look at working memory, such as the "digital span forward and backward," in which subjects are asked to remember sequences of digits rapidly presented to them. Farah also tried to explore how Adderall might affect what we think of as creativity, using tasks such as the "remote associations text," in which participants come up with one word that links together three different words, and, as well, the "group embedded figures task," which asks subjects to identify a small pattern within a larger, more intricate geometric design. These are the kinds of tasks with which attention—a notoriously baggy, catch-all term—is operationalized in labs.

On balance, Farah and others have found, again and again, very small to no improvement when their research subjects confront these tests of impulse control, memory, learning, and creativity while on Adderall. Ultimately, she suggests, it is possible that "lower-performing people actually do improve on the drug, and higher-performing people show no effect or actually get worse."

What Adderall clearly does extremely well is make people *think* they are doing better—and to feel good while they're doing it. "Adderall might not be a cognitive enhancement drug, but a 'drive' drug," says Anjan Chatterjee, a professor of neurology at the University of Pennsylvania's medical school. Farah explains, "[Stimulants] make boring work seem more interesting, so they increase your motivation to work, energy for work, and that's not nothing—that's really helpful . . . Unfortunately, it also gets into the realm of feel-good drugs, and that means the risk of dependence is quite high." Yet when I ask Farah exactly how addictive Adderall and other stimulant medications are, she tells me that there is currently no good answer. "Nobody has really looked at these drugs used as work enhancers and what the dependence risk there is," she said.

In retrospect, Farah says, the commentary published in *Nature* might have represented "the last hurrah in a flurry of optimism about the ability of drugs like Adderall to promote human flourishing." Yet she is careful to note that she and her colleagues were more intent on praising the *idea* of a drug like Adderall than they were trying to single out Adderall itself as a long-sought panacea for our modern woes. "Cognitive enhancement is not a bad thing, in and of itself," she said.

For Chatterjee, the use of Adderall off-label is comparable to plastic surgery: no less, and no more, existentially troubling. At Columbia, Carl Hart tells me that, to his way of thinking, it makes more sense for a person "who knows what they're doing" to take a small dose of Adderall than to rely on caffeine. Fewer headaches. Fewer calories.

I tried several times to get off the drug. Each attempt began the same way. Step 1: the rounding up of all the pills in my possession, including those secret stashes hidden away in drawers and closets, even in neglected corners of my childhood home, where I had surreptitiously filed some away, as if preparing a doomsday readiness protocol. I would debate for hours whether to keep just one for "emergencies." Then the leap of faith and the flushing of the pills down the toilet. Step 2: a day or two of feeling all right, as if I could manage this after all. Step 3: a bleak slab of time when the effort needed to get through even the simple tasks of a single day felt stupendous, where the future stretched before me like a grim series of obligations I was far too tired to carry out. All work on my book would stop. Panic would set in. Then, an internal Adderall voice would take over, and I would jump up from my desk and scurry out to refill my prescription—almost always a simple thing to achieve— or borrow pills from a friend, if need be. And the cycle would begin again. Those moments were all shrouded in secrecy and shame. Very few people in my life knew the extent to which I worried that the drug had come to define me.

Occasionally, I'd read through the message boards on the websites devoted to Adderall addiction, the anonymous, disembodied voices crying out for help, or even just recognition, on the Internet. Some of these testimonies pierced through my fog, their terms so familiar. One mother, on QuittingAdderall.com, wrote:

> This is my first post, and my first time ever admitting that I have a severe addiction. I have to stop. I started taking adderall in OCT 2010. And my story isn't much different than most . . . The honeymoon period, then all downhill. I feel like I can not remember who I was, or how it felt, to go one minute of the day not on adderall. I look back at pictures of myself from before this began and I wonder how I was ever "happy" without it bc now I am a nervous wreck if I even come close to not having my pills for the day. There have been nights I have cried laying my

daughter down to sleep because I was so ashamed that the time she spent with her mommy that day wasn't real . . . And I still didn't stop.

Testimonies of being trapped in the addiction—living a life that "wasn't real," as this mother felt she was doing—were as familiar to me as the descriptions of the hell of getting clean. Another:

The way I feel now is way worse than my ADD ever was before I went on this stuff. I no longer feel, at this present time, able to get a PhD. I don't feel able to do coursework, I don't feel interested and passionate about the things I loved. I need to know from you, dear readers, that this will be temporary.

I stayed in this cycle, using Adderall even as I saw with growing clarity that it was an impediment to all the things I valued most: reading, writing, friendship, love. Stopping it for a day, two days, a week. Then, feeling miserable, getting back on. I was stuck, panicky, and nothing reflected the problem more clearly than the state of the book I was still, four years later, trying desperately to finish. It was, by now, past due to its publisher. I had managed to turn in one draft, but my editor wasn't happy with it. In fact, she didn't respond at all for months. When I finally managed to get a meeting with her, what she said was this: "It needs more YOU!" Specifics were not forthcoming. Scared of losing the book after all these years of working on it, I went back to my computer and tried to inject into this story of Freudian ideas and neuroscientific findings plenty of colorful, twentysomething details. I knew that I wasn't thinking clearly inside my private Adderall reality, but I also felt I couldn't stop taking the pills *now,* mid-salvage. After all these years swallowing them down, I had lost confidence in my natural attention.

In the meantime, my editor quit to take a job at a different publishing company and I turned over my strange, lumpen manuscript to the new editor assigned to me, a young woman who edited health and wellness books. I was concerned about this match, aware that she and I might not share a creative outlook. And, early in 2013, in the middle of a gloriously white New York City blizzard, she met me at a downtown bakery and canceled my book, explaining that, in essence, "it just doesn't need to exist."

Obviously, that was a serious problem. I couldn't seem to conjure up a suitable defense while sitting in that silent bakery, where it felt that every table was occupied by a stylish downtown New Yorker eavesdropping on my humiliation. The meeting was over in a matter of minutes. My editor had to get home before the subways closed for the blizzard.

The next morning, my niece Lucy was born. The streets were piled with glistening white snow as I rushed to New York Hospital to meet her. *Needing to exist.* I looked at this perfect new baby as my former editor's words went round and round in my brain, my neurons fighting to tamp down the shock of her verdict.

The next six weeks were difficult ones. The canceled manuscript went out to every publisher in New York, making its rounds, its desperation apparent. Every publisher said no. And then, in the first weeks of spring, an email came, from an editor I had heard so much about, asking if I could come in and meet with him. This was a person who had edited a long list of extraordinary authors, many of whom I greatly admired. Therefore, I was not optimistic. But I woke up on the morning of our meeting and thought: I *can't* show up on Adderall. Better to be lethargic, exhausted, even *fighting sleep,* than on this drug. I never wanted to have to wonder: Could this have worked out if I hadn't been on drugs that day?

I was shown into a small conference room. I arranged my winter coat on the back of the chair and slid down into the seat, across from two of New York's great editors. And what can I say? If I were to make a list of the best conversations of my life, this would undoubtedly be one of them. What we talked about, mainly, were books that we loved, and why. It was a conversation that depended on being able to remember the fine-grain details of storytelling, the details that float back into your mind as unpredictably as inspiration itself. At one point, talking about the book *Mountains Beyond Mountains,* by Tracy Kidder, I remarked on one endearing detail in particular: a moment involving a pineapple Life Saver. In the book, it's a detail so small, so outside the larger narrative, that I hadn't thought of it in years. And yet, it is one of the book's most humanizing moments, and it made us all smile. It was like a pledge of some kind, a statement that we saw and loved the same things.

And for whatever it's worth: I am quite sure that no pineapple Life Saver would have come into my mind that day if I had come into that room on Adderall.

At the end of the hour, there was a provisional offer. If I were willing to re-report and significantly revise the manuscript—it would take me a year to execute the new concept they had for it—they *might* do this book with me. I staggered out. I was thirty years old. I had been ensnared by these pills for more than a decade, endlessly obsessing about the question of attention, wanting more, convinced my natural capacities did not suffice.

Yet that conviction had led me profoundly astray. Now what I thought was: if I squander this moment by continuing on with the pills, then god help me, I don't deserve any more chances, more luck, or grace. Call it what you will.

But there was a second force propelling me to end my relationship with amphetamines: I had a brilliant psychiatrist. We had, by now, been discussing Adderall for going on two years. We had talked and talked, about creativity, authenticity, and emotion. On the wall in her office, she had a single image: a framed print of a Matisse painting. Throughout our sessions, Matisse became a charmed concept between us, a name we invoked in a special tone of voice. He stood for the creative process: you start one place, go through hell, and wind up somewhere else, somewhere that surprises you. Adderall, we both agreed, was a perversion of that journey. In the end, it was the personal crisis of having my book canceled, and the offer of a second chance, that provided the prompt for quitting. But it was the conversations I had with this doctor that I seized upon to do it, her words that sustained me. I believe she saved my life.

During the first weeks of finally being off, the fatigue was as real as it had been before, the effort required to run even a tiny errand momentous, the gym unthinkable. The cravings were a force of their own: if someone so much as said "Adderall" in my presence, I would instantly begin to scheme about how to get just one more pill. Or maybe two. I was anxious a lot of the time, terrified I had done something irreversible to my brain, terrified that I was going to discover that I couldn't write without my special pills. But even in these first faltering weeks, there were immediate consolations. Simple pleasures were available to me again. I laughed more in conversation with my friends, and I noticed that they did too. I had spent years of my life in a state of false intensity, always wondering if I should be somewhere else, working harder, achieving more. In the deep lethargy of withdrawal, I could shed that chemical urgency that kept me at a subtle distance from everyone around me.

By the 4th of July, I was done, across some invisible threshold, standing on the other side of the stream. But, once across, I couldn't help but see that at some point during my Adderall decade, the way we *all* pay attention had changed. Driven by the proliferation of digital devices in our lives, the new norm was to shift rapidly from one source of information to the next, from one long article to the text message that arrives while we're reading it, to the sudden realization that we never replied to our friend's email about supporting her with a donation as she runs the New York City Marathon, to the impulse to first check our credit card balance before we do so—at which point the original text is abandoned, forgotten, and we are left disoriented, blindly reacting to whatever else the day blows in. Faced with a page of words, my brain now itched for dispatches via computer screens, anything to interrupt my own train of thought.

It had become commonplace to attend a movie and look out to see that several in the audience were unable to resist the ghostly glow of their personal screen lives for the duration of the film. On the highway, it seemed exotic to spot a driver who wasn't looking at her phone, even when driving a car full of children. In my neighborhood, I saw strollers with an attachment that allowed mothers to place their phones between themselves and their babies, so what their eyes looked to first was not the reciprocal gaze of their own infants, but rather their small screen, presenting them with the daily flow of ephemera. The conversations I had with friends at dinner tables were constantly interrupted by the arrival of messages, however trivial, from people who were not in the room.

The very conveniences that were supposed to be making our

lives easier, more efficient and more connected, were often, it seemed, having the opposite effect: bewildering us with their ability to rob us of our hours, presenting us with the alienating fact that the people we know and love have a second version of themselves, the ones represented on screens. In the same way that Adderall, an attention drug, had for me and for many people I encountered divested us of our actual powers of attention, so too had our technology come to make life feel more overwhelming, not less. In the great maw of our chirping screens, I felt all my old loves, all my old values, rumble on their foundations.

It struck me that this new pattern of splintered concentration and constant interruption made it seem that everyone around me had an attention disorder, that everyone was now a candidate for the Adderall cure. I was off the Adderall now, but I had a whole new task, a whole new question to answer. Stripped of my pills in an age of distraction, what did it even mean to pay attention?

3

But I do want to say a little more about the Adderall. Specifically, about the first months of being off, hellish and thrilling as they were. In the spring of 2013, as I was trimming back my dose and skipping more and more pills entirely, I was often tired and apathetic, but an even more daunting fact also revealed itself. A day without Adderall was *endless*. For so long, I had popped a pill in order to override my own biological rhythms with whatever Shire pharmaceuticals wanted me to feel. Now I was defenseless against the ups and downs, responsible for my own approach to each morning, afternoon, and night.

And then there was the writing. My new editor had an idea for how to fix my book, one we both agreed felt right. It was to flesh out the story of a group of psychoanalysts working with very difficult patients. These were patients not usually considered eligible for psychoanalysis. They had suffered through accidents, strokes, and other conditions that left them with the kind of brain damage that is normally considered well outside the purview of psychologizing. But this particular group of analysts believed no one was more urgently in need of psychological help than exactly these patients, who were often profoundly isolated, stuck in wheelchairs or assisted living, their ability to communicate severely damaged by the damage to their brains.

I agreed that for my book to be complete, I should choose one of the psychoanalysts and report in detail on the work he or she was doing. There was one member of the group who stood out to me as the obvious choice. He was a slight man, white-haired, with a raspy, humorous, Bronx-bred voice, who dressed casually and emanated warmth. His patient had had a stroke ten years before, which had left him intellectually intact but severely aphasic. Meaning he couldn't speak. This, then, was the talking cure carried out with a patient who could not talk.

I tracked down this therapist's number online and called him at home one snowy evening, in the suburbs of Long Island, to ask if he would be interested in opening up his work to me for the book I was writing. Without skipping a beat, he replied in his raspy voice: "This is kind of cramping my style. You see, I have cancer." Yet moments later, he was opening up his datebook to find a time to begin.

This was the man I would call David Silvers. It was not his real name, but one of his major concerns was how to protect his patient's privacy, even though his patient had given permission for his case to be used in writing. David wanted to add extra layers of disguise, not only changing his patient's name and other identifying features, but changing his own name on top of that. That was his wish when he was alive; I carry it forward here.

By the time his patient, Arthur, began to see David, he had created a whole new routine to cope with his Broca's aphasia. Before the stroke, he'd been a fortysomething exercise nut who lived downtown, maybe with a lover, maybe not—David wasn't entirely sure. Details were not always reliable, or, rather, communicable. Now Arthur usually arrived at David's office on a cane, his mobility severely impaired by the stroke. Now he lived alone.

As commonly occurs with Broca's aphasia, Arthur had only a handful of words available to him, often uttered in an excitable staccato: *yes yes yes yes yes.* Or: *laminada,* the string of nonsense syllables that could stand in for countless different meanings. The problem in Broca's aphasia is not with speaking per se: it is with expressing, with getting out the intended meaning in any form, oral or written.

Besides his limited spoken vocabulary, Arthur's other means of communication was a yellow legal pad on which he was able to scrawl clumps of letters or messy sketches, little half-realized diagrams composed of simple lines and shapes. He and David passed the paper back and forth between them as David would patiently, arduously decode Arthur's writing. When he got it wrong, Arthur shook with frustration. When he got it right: *yes yes yes yes yes.* And, often, that affirmation came with an expression on Arthur's face that meant: *What took you so long?* The contents of their session were rooted in the quotidian, a reconstruction of Arthur's week, his routine, all the concrete practicalities that now filled his time.

I saw something that looked like "Babel" scrawled on the page in Arthur's writing.

"Well, it's a Russian author, but I suspect that's not what we're talking about here," David said, pointing to some adjacent syllables. "My guess right now? Is Bloomingdale's. Because

he likes to dress well, and he goes to good places. That could be
an attempt at Bloomingdale's, I'm serious."

Every once in awhile, the conversation would tip into emotion, Arthur slumped in his chair, or pointing up at the ceiling,
a gesture that David quickly came to understand. *I want to die
already.*

David had kept all of these yellow pad pages, each one of
them covered in evocative half-words and symbols, like some
kind of treasure map. On the back, David had stapled his own
detailed notes from that day's session. Now they added up to a
thick dossier he kept on a shelf in the little den we sat in. Each
week, we went through exactly one session, or maybe two.
David didn't want to skip a single detail, a single emotional note
or inference. David had been seeing Arthur for more than five
years by the time I showed up. The case had in some real sense
been the highlight of his career as a therapist, the most difficult,
most rewarding feat he'd ever undertaken.

Attention is the rarest and purest form of generosity. The French
writer, philosopher, and mystic Simone Weil wrote that. Weil's
words often came to my mind as I sat across from David. It
seemed to me he was actually practicing something different
from the "evenly hovering attention" Freud had prescribed as
the ideal analytic stance. But it was the quality of David's attention, his endless attention, to the details of Arthur's life that kept
his patient coming back, week after week, for half a decade.
There were now so few people in Arthur's life willing or able
to do the same.

David's generosity extended to everyone, not only those he
saw professionally. He treated me with unflagging gentleness,
receiving my every question with respect and enthusiasm, no
matter how truly uninformed I sounded. He inserted kindness where I wouldn't have guessed kindness could go. If I

reached over to help him turn on the lamp: "Oh, good for you, that's a tricky one." He did not know, of course, that on those weekly visits, especially in the first months together, I was often exhausted, struggling not to feel overwhelmed by how gray and monolithic the world looked from the perspective of chemical withdrawal. I was raw and uncertain of my strength. He was too: the cancer treatments he'd been going through had taken so much out of him. Some days he felt so limited, he'd greet me in his robe. We would retreat to his little den, sit facing each other, and take solace in the connection he had forged with his patient, his campaign to redeem every detail of another person's life.

Just as spring turned into summer, I began to date an Englishman named Andrew. I had first met him years before, when we were both in Los Angeles at the same time, visiting our friends, who happened to be friends with each other. We all had lunch one day at a 1950s-themed diner in West Hollywood. To me, Andrew was as attractive as he was unavailable. He gazed out the diner's window throughout the meal, apparently absorbed by the palm trees on Beverly Boulevard.

Now, six years later, I was heading to his apartment in Brooklyn, where he was going to make me dinner. He struck me as a true exotic, perched in his book-lined apartment in a charming old walk-up, where he cooked expertly in his small kitchen— salmon and corn on the cob and three different vegetables. But in the days to follow, I began to notice a pattern. Together we seemed to zigzag in and out of intimacy; one moment, Andrew was charming and engaged, the next withering, or witheringly absent. I was always wounded by these lapses into disconnection, blaming myself and my own conversational shortcomings, my own lack of worthy content. After our nights together, I might or might not hear from him. He might reply right away to a text message, or he might wait for days. Yet something drew me back, again and again. It was the beginning of summer, the days were glorious, and I couldn't believe I had so much energy to burn. I had been sure that without Adderall, I would live my whole life in a half torpor. Instead, I was putting on sundresses and racing to Brooklyn, taking the stairs two at a time all the way up to the top.

Andrew had planned to spend the summer traveling abroad. The night before his departure, we sat out at a sidewalk café. He was leaving, but I was bound to my desk in New York, to take my best swing at fixing all that was wrong with my book. Except for one major trip: I had decided to go to South Africa that August, to attend a conference where David had been invited to speak about his work with Arthur. I was going, despite the expense, because David had vowed to make the nearly twenty-hour flight, though he was by that time tremendously weakened by his cancer treatments. He felt compelled to present the work he was doing to his colleagues in the hope that they would feel empowered to take on similarly impossible cases. I knew I had to be in the audience to see him take that stage.

"I'd come with you to Africa if you'd invite me," Andrew finally said, after two rounds of mojitos. I was elated; we vowed to meet in six weeks, in the Johannesburg airport. As soon as we concocted this plan, it bound us together through the ensuing weeks of absence, as he disappeared into Europe. In some sense, I suppose, Andrew neatly replaced Adderall in my own personal constellation of preoccupations: instead of investing to the point of obsession in a small round pill, I now transferred the full force of my attention onto him. I fantasized about him for hours every day, imagining every detail of our upcoming trip, the clothes I would wear, the book I would bring as a gift, the inscription I would write in it, which I practiced on a piece of paper ten times before committing to. My supercharged invest-ment in Andrew, or the idea of Andrew, was painful, and it wasted many, many hours of my life, but there was a part of me that considered it healthy, like coming back to the world of sensuality and passion after a decade of amphetamine-induced detachment. I don't know if I recognized then how much my Adderall thinking was still alive and well in this burgeoning relationship, even in the absence of the pills themselves. And Andrew himself was like a drug: in his company I felt high, not at all myself, removed from the rest of my life. It wasn't love; it was something other. A kind of unholy, animal bond existed between us.

We did meet in the Johannesburg airport, just as we'd said. It was early in the morning and we'd both come off long flights when we found each other in the customs line. Emerging into baggage claim, we came upon a bizarre scene: a middle-aged white man screaming at a small group of black airport atten-dants. He was beside himself, like a child having a full-body meltdown. He was screaming so loudly it was difficult to make out his words. Andrew thought he was saying "You've lost my kids." I heard "You've lost my guns." We had arrived in South Africa.

For the next two weeks, we roamed the country. In the absence of Adderall, my senses felt utterly unblocked, porous, soaking up the vivid details of the country around me. Nearly every scenario we found ourselves in struck me as rich material for a short story. And, actually, I often had to look at it like that: with a writer's detachment, because the experience of being with Andrew was such an anxious one for me. I was forever worrying about his mood, his inner state. When the day of the conference rolled around, I was more worried about the contents of Andrew's mind than I was focused on David's presentation. My attention felt utterly out of my own control.

When I got back to New York, I called my best friend from the taxi I took home from the airport. I seem to remember crying, and telling her "I am not optimistic." But it took until well past Labor Day for me to finally extricate myself from Andrew. On our last night together, I was back in his Brooklyn apartment. Everything felt wrong, off, the disconnected bits so much more frequent than our easy, close moments. This was true even though that very night, he was inviting me for a long weekend with his friends to a lake house, and uttering such uninspiring sentences as "Of course you're my *girlfriend.*" When he went to brush his teeth, I picked up his phone and found exactly what, I suppose, I had expected to find: a correspondence with a girl named Rosa, with whom he'd had so much fun square-dancing in Bryant Park the week before, and really wanted to see again, and was she free this week?

I put the phone down. I lay on Andrew's bed. He emerged from the bathroom and handed me a stapled printout of the novelist David Foster Wallace's well-loved commencement speech, often referred to as "This Is Water." Wallace had delivered the speech at Kenyon College in 2005, the only commencement speech he ever gave. "Have you ever read this one, then?" Andrew asked me. No, I hadn't. "Read it aloud," he said. So I did, from beginning to end.

Wallace is telling the Kenyon kids what he thinks they need to know as they head out into adulthood. What he wants to talk about, specifically, is not the usual stuff of the commencement speech, but rather, the utterly concrete, banal, day-in-and-day-out details of life as it's lived. He's most interested in the situation where you find yourself at your job, and it's the end of the day, and you're tired, and you're hungry, but you realize you don't have any food at home, and you're going to have to sit in rush-hour traffic and get to the crowded grocery store and deal with all the dreary logistics to be found there: how bored and frustrated it's possible to be. ". . . because my natural default setting is the certainty that situations like this are really all about *me,* about my hungriness and my fatigue and my desire to just get home, and it's going to seem, for all the world, like everybody else is *just in my way . . .*"

Addressing these twentysomethings, who still don't really know about the texture of getting up in the morning and going to work and going to the grocery store and coming home and repeating the whole relentless thing again and again for the rest of their lives, Wallace is trying to say there's a way out—or through—that isn't talked about nearly enough. Rather than sit in rush-hour traffic and fume at the obnoxious SUVs wasting space and resources, he writes, "it's not impossible that some of these people in SUVs have been in horrible auto accidents in the past, and now find driving so terrifying that their therapist has all but ordered them to get a huge, heavy SUV so they can feel safe enough to drive. Or that the Hummer that just cut me off is maybe being driven by a father whose little child is hurt or sick in the seat next to him, and he's trying to get this kid to the hospital, and he's in a way bigger, more legitimate hurry than I am—it is actually *I* who am in *his* way. Or I can choose to force myself to consider the likelihood that everyone else in the supermarket's checkout line is just as bored and frustrated as I am, and that some of these people probably have harder, more tedious and painful lives than I do."

This is the kind of exercise in attention he is asking the students to consider, the imaginative leap he is asking them to take. "If you've really learned how to think, how to pay attention," he tells them, "then you will know you have other options. It will actually be within your power to experience a crowded, hot, slow, consumer-hell type situation as not only meaningful, but sacred, on fire with the same force that lit the stars—love, fellowship, the mystical oneness of all things deep down."

I read the whole speech out loud to Andrew, not able then, yet, to fully engage with Wallace's meaning, so shell-shocked and self-conscious and even self-loathing was I, that I was clearly so inferior to the fabulous, free-spirited Rosa, square-dancing the night away. Yet I sensed a world of meaning waiting for me in what Wallace had written, and who Wallace was, despite his complications, his all-too-pronounced imperfections, his deep and ongoing struggle to live the very values of respect and empathy that he prescribed to others. I didn't know anything about any of that then.

With visions of square-dancing Rosa in my head, I barely slept. And yet, I didn't storm out, or even slink. I lay there and thought about whether or not my intense sense of betrayal was actually justified. After all, I was the wretched snoop in this scenario. How dare I go through his phone? In the morning, when Andrew woke up, I told him what I had found. He denied everything and left for work. "I have to go to my *job* now" were his actual last words to me that day. I lay down again and dozed on his blanket. Then I got up and wrote a letter, in the wild, devolved handwriting of a Microsoft Word user, saying good-bye to him.

In the weeks after this unfortunate scene, I finally sat down to face the book. I was reeling from my time with Andrew, and unnerved by the deadline fast approaching. But when I tried to get to work, it was hell. It was actually harder than I thought it was going to be. The issue wasn't concentration, necessarily. It was the searing self-doubt that Adderall had in some ways helped me to ignore, and which now rose up like a tidal wave, pounding me from every angle. Or maybe this *was* an issue of concentration after all: the ability to drown out all competing voices, to sit with the agonizing task at hand and not look away. I was flooded with thoughts I couldn't control, as if my mind had to relearn the principle of selection after so many years on its unnatural diet. W. H. Auden, great English poet and Benzedrine devotee, had this to say on the subject: "Choice of attention—to pay attention to this and ignore that—is to the inner life what choice of action is to the outer. In both cases, a man is responsible for his choice and must accept the consequences, whatever they may be." If you like, you can order these words etched onto a wooden plaque. It will cost you $19.99 on Amazon. Far more difficult is to internalize its message: that attention is a decision, a muscle to be strengthened and flexed.

And the fall of 2013 found mine in an atrophied state. I had forgotten what it meant to rely on my natural ability to focus. I was, in fact, entirely estranged from my own attention. I spent difficult hours at the Writers Room, the downtown writing space I belonged to, surrounded by other writers, many of whom were undoubtedly having their own silent freak-outs at their own laptops. I wondered who among them might also be on pills, or trying not to be on pills. I envied the serene-looking ones, who showed up day after day and typed away untroubled by a private war against drugs, who couldn't imagine doing to themselves what I had done, which was to obscure my inner state—the single greatest resource for any writer—with a fog of chemical falsity.

Often, all I did manage to do was to sit there, my computer open in front of me, unable to muster the nerve to tackle the actual writing. What I did write, I despised. But I knew I had to keep typing, to establish new habits, new Pavlovian associations. I willed my neuroplasticity to kick in, my brain to learn new firing patterns. All the while I was sucked helplessly back into a recurrent set of dark thoughts. I ruminated on the wreckage of Andrew. I continued from there on to thoughts about the mess I'd made inside my own skull. I was convinced that I had wreaked such havoc on my neurons with a decade of too much Adderall that I would not manage to find my way. Simply for the sake of writing something, anything, I would open a Word document to document the agony. I look through my old journals now from that time period. My mental health was far from optimal. On the other hand, it could have been worse.

September 23, 2013

IT IS ABSOLUTELY BREATHTAKING HOW MUCH I WANT ADDERALL RIGHT NOW. I am quite simply talking myself almost to the point of figuring out how to get the refill, considering I ripped up my old prescription paper last week. I could call the doctor and tell him I lost the script and could he write out a new one. I could do that. I could, I could. But I won't. Not now. Not yet.

October 24, 2013

List of all concerns:
Loss of youth, failure to have enjoyed youth while I still could.
Permanent brain damage from years of adderall, a dulling of the senses, a lowering of my IQ, all the experiences I failed to have.
Promiscuity.
Credit card debt.
My clothes are completely wrong. But completely.

I am not in love with anybody & nobody is in love with me.

Future of journalism.

Failure to separate properly from my family, esp my parents

Did the hazelnut ice coffee I just sucked down actually contain hazelnut SYRUP?

It was November before I began to write, to really write— seven months after meeting my new editor, eight months after the beginning of the end of Adderall, four months after being entirely off the drug. My mantra as I began to type each day: "I can always erase this." I thought about unhelpful things that made me feel bad, like the fact that I was pursuing a form of work that seemed to occupy less and less a place of value in our digital age. That I had been at work on it for years, relegated to the lonely silence of the Writers Room, as everyone I knew was gravitating to texts that did not exceed 140 characters, that disappeared from view faster than invisible ink.

I continued to see David. Well into 2014, I would borrow my father's car and drive up the Long Island Expressway. As we edged closer to the end of David's stack of yellow legal pad pages, he in turn seemed to slow down his narration. I thought of Scheherazade, stretching out her stories to make them last as long as she could. Over those months, David was getting weaker and weaker.

In one of our final meetings, I remember puttering around in his kitchen, making him a simple lunch, as it had become hard for him now to stand up. From his chair, he sat talking to me about how much he loved his family, laughing and smiling, cracking jokes, as he always did. He had seen me through Andrew and the dissolution of Andrew. He had even met Andrew, in South Africa. And, not long after I told him Andrew and I were through, David turned to me in the middle of one of our sessions, wanting to weigh in for a second on the question of marriage.

"You get up in the morning and you look who you're with," he said, from his sofa. "I don't mean beauty. I mean, who am I *with*?"

David died five months before my book was published, which it was, just before I turned thirty-three. But he read every page on which he was mentioned. To this day, when I think about the value, about the sheer power of attention paid from one human being to another, I think about David and Arthur, those sheets of yellow legal pad paper, that monumental effort to understand.

4

Another David. Consider this David, if only briefly. Though can one be brief on a subject like David Foster Wallace? His output in terms of page numbers alone so exceeds his short life, it is hard to know where to begin. And yet. David Foster Wallace was someone who thought constantly about attention. On this subject, Wallace took an unusual tack: he emphasized the ethics of how we choose to guide our thoughts, moment to moment. And, as well, the *stakes*. Wallace thought that attention could save your life, although, in the end, it did not save his own.

At Kenyon, in 2005, giving his commencement speech, Wallace told the kids: "learning how to think really means learning how to exercise some control over how and what you think. It means being conscious and aware enough to choose what you pay attention to and to choose how you construct meaning from experience. Because if you cannot exercise this kind of choice in adult life, you will be totally hosed."

Wallace died three years later, taking his life at his home

in Claremont, California, losing the long, brutal battle with depression that had begun when he was a teenager. But the great big theme of attention that he chose to dedicate his speech to had in fact been on his mind, and in his work, long before he stood at that college lectern to address the graduating seniors. Wallace—in different periods of his life a television binge watcher, competitive tennis player, math and logic whiz, and devourer of information—laced themes of attention and distraction throughout much of his work.

I may as well confess: I made it through *Infinite Jest* only recently, though it has sat on my shelf for years. And, actually, it was one of the mightiest feats of attention I have attempted in the last decade. I read it through the dog days of August in New York City, schlepping it onto humid subway platforms, propping it up awkwardly on my lap as I sought respite on sweaty sofa cushions, setting for myself a fifty-page daily minimum to ensure I would at least get *somewhere* with it by Labor Day.

Just under a thousand pages long (to say nothing of the endnotes, to say nothing of the footnotes that accompany many of the endnotes), it is a book written, in one sense, for a pre-iPhone brain, minutely detailed, endlessly populated, a novel that moves in millimeters. In an interview, Wallace once likened his writing style to "an enormous eyeball floating around something, reporting what it sees." On the other hand, *Infinite Jest* is perfectly, almost uncannily suited for our digital age, its fragmented narrative jumping from one stream of ideas to the next. Wallace mirrors back to us exactly the kind of splintered thinking we've now grown used to through all the hours we spend online.

To my surprise, the experience of reading this book, the radical commitment it required, imbued those weeks of my life with a charged atmosphere, a special, elevated quality that took me outside the wearying ephemera to be found on my various screens and transported me back to an earlier time, before I could have even imagined a thing like Instagram. Though not Wallace: he knew what was coming. In *Infinite Jest,* he imagines a world in which people sat at home watching on-demand programming delivered over the "interlace," "pulsed in," filling their homes with compulsively diverting entertainments.

Infinite Jest was published in 1996, the same year that two Stanford students named Larry Page and Sergey Brin began the research project that would soon produce Google. Microsoft had just launched Internet Explorer. It was also the year that Adderall hit the American market. Much of the book's action takes place in the near future, in the fictional town of Enfield, Massachusetts (*Have you ever been to Enfield?*), in two locales: a tennis academy for teenagers and a halfway house for down-and-out adults. Tennis and addiction—in both cases, Wallace wrote from direct experience.

In *Infinite Jest,* the tennis academy sits on top of the hill; the halfway house, down in the shadows below it. There is also, somehow, a squadron of legless, wheelchair-bound Quebecois separatist assassins. They are seeking an infamous weapon of war: a video cartridge, called "Infinite Jest," that is so extremely, so universally entertaining, those watching simply cannot look away. Mesmerized, they are rooted in place, they soil themselves, they do not sleep or eat. They have to be carted away to institutions where they live out their days in a state of vegetative blankness. Either that or they simply remain in place, eyes glued to the screen, stuck in their chair, where, pretty soon, they die.

One of these legless assassins, Rémy Marathe, provides the book's most pointed commentary on the American obsession with being constantly entertained. Marathe is the book's moral arbiter, questioning the American habit of entrancing ourselves so promiscuously, so indiscriminately. "Choose with care," he says. "You are what you love. No?"

It was clear to Wallace that we were, for the most part, utterly failing in this task. To be careful, to be deliberate about what we embrace. About where we spend our precious attention.

Actually, I do not believe there is anything accidental or incidental about the twinning of Wallace's two great themes: attention and addiction. It has taken me a long time to understand how deeply interconnected they are. It has taken me, in fact, getting to know Wallace's work to understand the connection. They both have everything to do with being able to sit with yourself; to bear the often dull, sometimes agonizing task of just sitting with yourself.

By the time I read *Infinite Jest,* I may have gotten off the Adderall, but I still hadn't answered the question underlying that whole addicted decade. I didn't even know what it was, didn't see that what I was asking was this: Is my natural-born attention possibly enough? Is it going to be enough? Every time I took a pill, I was answering *no,* of course. But even long after I stopped, even as I type these words now, I am still asking that same question.

After the publication of *Infinite Jest,* Wallace told the journalist David Lipsky: "The technology's gonna get better and better at doing what it does, which is seduce us into being incredibly dependent on it, so that advertisers can be more confident that we will watch their advertisements." Lipsky, a brainy young writer from New York, had come to write a profile of Wallace for *Rolling Stone.* Which was fitting, because, with the appearance of *Infinite Jest,* Wallace was now almost as rock-star famous as a novelist could get. During that week together, the two Davids, both in their thirties, traveled around the Midwest in cars and planes and said deep things to each other, while Lipsky smoked and Wallace spat his endless stream of chewing tobacco into a series of different tin cans. "It's gonna get easier and easier, and more and more convenient, and more and more pleasurable, to be alone with images on a screen, given to us by people who do not love us but want our money," Wallace continued. "Which is all right. In low doses, right? But if that's the basic main staple of your diet, you're gonna die. In a meaningful way, you're gonna die."

Gradually, the explicit emphasis on addiction faded from his work, but Wallace never stopped writing about attention. By his forties, he'd become interested in meditation and Eastern thought, themes of which—awareness, compassion, freedom—so clearly animate "This Is Water." I saw why, inevitably, Wallace would have gravitated to the ancient Eastern techniques. He needed to escape his own mind. And the great promise of meditation is that you can: by paying close attention to your mind, to the moods and thoughts it produces, you gradually learn that you are not identical with those moods and thoughts. Pay attention "ardently." So instructs the Buddha to the meditator. So, in his way, did Wallace instruct those Kenyon kids, in the years that followed.

But Wallace struggled with the practice. His biographer D. T. Max reports that Wallace stumbled on the fine print. "Is it OK to sit in a chair? Or is severe pain part of the (non) point?" he once asked an experienced meditator. "Is it half-lotus or nothing? If so, why?" Wallace enrolled in a two-week meditation course in Plum Village, France, run by the Buddhist monk and author Thich Nhat Hanh. Wallace left early. He wrote to his friend Don DeLillo, blaming the food.

It wasn't the first time Wallace had tried to become an adherent. Googling "David Foster Wallace" and "God" one day, I find a beautiful essay on *Christianity Today*'s website, written by Warren Cole Smith. Smith is writing on the tenth anniversary of Wallace's death, describing an underappreciated aspect of Wallace's life: his attraction to faith, his desire to believe. Wallace's father, a professor, was a passionate atheist, writes Smith, but Wallace was attracted to religion, regularly watched religious programs on television, and tried, at least once, to join the Catholic Church. But "he had too many questions." When he got into AA, he was faced with similar questions, now in the form of the requirement: "to surrender to a power higher than ourselves." Whatever he may have felt about that admonishment, however unrealistic or "cliché," Wallace stayed clean.

After Wallace's suicide, at the age of forty-six, his longtime editor at Little, Brown, Michael Pietsch, scraped together the manuscript pages Wallace had been working on at the time of his death. Which, it's worth mentioning, Wallace had left in a neat enough arrangement for Pietsch to assemble into a book. *The Pale King,* a novel that takes place in the world of the IRS, was published in 2011. It is a book about taxes and tedium. To my mind, it is the culmination of years of thought about the power of attention in defining a human life.

In fact, while reading *The Pale King,* it was impossible not to notice that for long stretches at a time, the word "attention" seemed to pop up on almost every page. Indeed, according to at least one tally, "attention" appears 150 times in Wallace's final work of fiction. David Wallace himself is a character in his book, cropping up sporadically. "Author, here," he likes to begin. On one of these occasions he offers what I consider to be the keystone passage, the question driving every line of his final book: "why we recoil from the dull."

"Maybe dullness is associated with psychic pain because something that's dull or opaque fails to provide enough stimulation to distract people from some other, deeper type of pain that is always there," he writes. ". . . I can't think anyone really believes that today's so-called 'information society' is just about information. Everyone knows it's about something else, way down."

This "something else" that Wallace alludes to, this something else that "everyone knows it's about." A moment to pause and consider what he meant by this. Why are we so susceptible to all the escape routes our technologies offer us in the first place? What are we fleeing? In many ways, as I thought about attention, I realized that this was the question I cared most about, the single question I wanted to answer. Or, at the very least, to ask.

I had nearly finished *The Pale King* when I went to visit Wallace's final residence. It was the only literary pilgrimage I'd ever undertaken. I drove from Los Angeles to Claremont, California, on a Monday afternoon in October, ten years and one month after his death, my dog-eared copy of his last published book on the shotgun seat of my rental car. I had found the address after a little Internet sleuthing. It was not the address invoked by Wallace as occasional narrator in *The Pale King*. ("David Wallace," he writes. "Age 40, SS no 975-04-2012, addressing you from my Form 8829-deductible home office at 725 Indian Hill Blvd, Claremont 91711 CA, on this fifth day of spring, 2005.") Rather, I was in search of the second house he lived in in Claremont, the one that was farther out of town, just beneath where the hills began.

Wallace had lived in this house with his wife, Karen Green,

an artist he married in his forties, a woman around his own age, who already had a teenage son when they met. Wallace had been engaged several times, but this was his only marriage. And, by all accounts, it was a good one, marking a largely peaceful phase in Wallace's life. He had moved to Claremont to teach creative writing at Pomona College. Now, instead of the fierce midwestern winters, he walked his big dogs in abundant West Coast sunshine all year long. And, actually, this is what I was thinking about when I arrived at the home he had shared with Green: the light. The five-o'clock liquid-gold sunlight, washing the whole sky, the whole street, in its forgiving glow. I couldn't help but think: How could he decide to say goodbye to this light?

Wallace and Green's place turned out to be a mid-century tract house, with pebbles out front and various succulents planted therein. The garage, I knew, had served as Wallace's office. And it was in the garage that Michael Pietsch found the trail Wallace had left for him, the trail of manuscript pages and computer files that would lead to the publishing of *The Pale King*. When I arrived, no one was home, it seemed, except for a dog, barking loudly, peering out at me in a canine hysteria from one uncovered portion of the living room window. The rest of the glass was concealed by a thin white curtain.

According to D. T. Max, it was while they lived in this house on this quiet, pretty, suburban street that Wallace and Green went out to dinner one night at a local Persian restaurant. Afterward, Wallace became sick. His doctor suggested taking him off the antidepressant he'd been on for decades, Nardil, because it had so many restrictions and side effects. The thinking here was that maybe Wallace had grown out of the depression by now and could function without meds or, at worst, replace the Nardil with a more modern alternative. And the thinking was catastrophic, it turned out. Off the Nardil for the first time in more than twenty years, Wallace walked straight into darkness, months and months of it. Even when he went back on the Nardil, it no longer worked as it had before. Nothing worked for him now. Toward the end, his parents came here to Claremont, to sit with him.

By then, Wallace had people with him almost all the time, keeping him company. But one day, after Wallace's parents had returned to Illinois, Green went out for a few hours, leaving him alone. When Green got home, she found that her husband had hanged himself on their patio.

"That he was blocked with his work when he decided to quit Nardil—was bored with his old tricks and unable to muster enough excitement about his new novel to find a way forward with it—is not inconsequential," writes Jonathan Franzen, in "Farther Away," the essay he published in *The New Yorker* a few years after Wallace's death. Franzen, an old friend, spent time with Wallace during the final summer of his life, coming to sit with him in Claremont, just as Wallace's parents did. At the time, Franzen was preparing to travel to Ecuador on a bird-watching trip. In Claremont, even in the face of Wallace's black depression, Franzen was busy learning the names of all the native birds he might see. He registered the chasm that now lay between himself and his old friend, who seemed to have lost the ability to care, to be interested by or absorbed in the world.

David had died of boredom. That was one of the conclusions Franzen reached while traveling to a remote island in the South Pacific known as Masafuera. He went there two years after Wallace's death, to look at birds, to read *Robinson Crusoe,* and to be alone—alone in the hope he might finally feel something other than rage about his friend's decision to take his own life. Boredom: the subject of Wallace's final book. The subject of so much of his thinking and writing. Had it done him in, in the end? Had his prodigious, almost superhuman attention failed him? Was it that he could no longer face what Simone Weil called "the horror of the void"? Or, Wallace himself: "the terror of silence." I knew it well, of course. The urge to shatter that silence, that boredom, to reach for our phones, our drugs, our achievements. *Everyone knows it's about something else, way down.*

Standing out on Oak Hollow Road, I felt a need to lay eyes on the patio where Wallace had died. The longer I stood on the street, the more powerful the impulse became. No one was home yet, except for the dog. But then a man appeared in the driveway next door, introducing himself. He had only moved in that summer. He hadn't known that David Foster Wallace lived next door. In fact, he was only vaguely familiar with Wallace's work, he said. But he was intrigued by my quest, and he allowed me to come into his backyard, where I stood on a little wooden chair and peered over the wall. From there, I was looking directly down onto Wallace's old patio. Nothing marked the spot, of course, at least nothing I could detect. It was a small paved area, an all-American tableau, with a covered barbeque and a string of twinkle lights attached to the single tree. Yet the sight of it was indescribably powerful.

Still on my lookout chair, I pulled out my phone and called my boyfriend, Josh. At that moment, he was in Los Angeles, doing something respectable, no doubt. "I want you to know I'm on a chair in a stranger's yard looking at the place where David Foster Wallace died," I told him. "Is this night going to end with me bailing you out of jail?" he asked me. I was aware how macabre this might seem, what I was doing, and how invasive. But somehow, it felt like paying homage, this effort, this futile effort to try to understand what had happened.

The reason, by the way, that Wallace's Kenyon commencement speech earned the title "This Is Water" is how it begins. "There are these two young fish swimming along and they happen to meet an older fish swimming the other way, who nods at them and says, 'Morning, boys. How's the water?' And the two young fish swim on for a bit, and then eventually one of them looks over at the other and goes 'What the hell is water?'

"If you're worried that I plan to present myself here as the wise, older fish explaining what water is to you younger fish, please don't be," Wallace continued that day at Kenyon. "The point of the fish story is merely that the most obvious, important realities are often the ones that are hardest to see and talk about."

This story, this parable, had been with Wallace a long time. It makes an appearance at the halfway point of *Infinite Jest,* published a decade earlier. It is spoken by a man named Robert F. outside an AA meeting, who speaks it while straddling his motorcycle, a girl behind him, her arms around his waist. He tells it to Don Gately, former addict-burglar, now sober resident of Ennet House, but still trying to find or even define his "higher power." As soon as Robert F. tells the parable, like the seasoned old fish himself, he departs, blasting away on his bike, leaving Don Gately there to ponder his meaning. *That the most obvious, important realities are often the ones that are hardest to see and talk about.*

———

I would say one other thing. As it happened, I bought my copy of *Infinite Jest* in January 2014, at a beautiful little bookstore called Three Lives & Company in Manhattan's West Village. As I handed it to the clerk, he asked me: "Is this a New Year's resolution?" His question prompted the man browsing the nearby table display to look up, seemingly to find out about what I might be purchasing. Out of the corner of my eye, I had actually assumed this man to be homeless, because he was so extremely disheveled, but more than that: so vulnerable, so completely down-and-out. When he raised his head at the clerk's question, though, I saw that it was the actor Philip Seymour Hoffman. The clerk and I seemed to process this information at the same time. We looked at each other, stunned. A week later, Hoffman was dead at forty-six, just like Wallace, found in his nearby apartment on Bethune Street with a needle in his arm, having returned to drugs after decades of sobriety. And I was back on Adderall.

It was one of the countless times I've temporarily slipped back into old patterns since the initial break from the drug, succumbing to the same wishful thinking that allowed me to enter into the addiction in the first place. Something like: Why not? Why not supercharge my system and live each day with boundless energy and ready-made focus? Why not override my own uncertain self with the guarantee of a chemical self? Each relapse doesn't last long, a few days maybe, never quite a week, but each time, I have to go back to the beginning, to review the reasons for amphetamine sobriety, the pounding, existential need to not be on this drug. These reasons include big-ticket items, like work, love, and authenticity. But also, even more immediately: *attention.* Because what I know by now, after all these nearly identical go-rounds, is that Adderall does nothing to enhance my ability to absorb the world, to intuit the essence, to, as Wallace recommends, imagine my way out of my own little predicament and into someone else's. On the contrary: Adderall directly impedes these very goals, erecting tight walls around me, boxing me into smallness, and causing me, again and again, to entirely miss the point.

Part II

A BRIEF HISTORY
OF WHAT MATTERS

5

So what, then, *is* the point? What is the reason to cultivate and devote one's single-minded attention? Is this kind of attention even still a possibility? Was it ever? In the years after Adderall, these were the questions I often thought about.

I approached from all angles. Walking the loop in Prospect Park, I listened to attention self-help books through my headphones, books such as *Deep Work* by Cal Newport and *Hyperfocus* by Chris Bailey. I was listening not in order to help myself (or so I believed), but, rather, to get a sense of the latest advice, and the language in which attention was now commodified. Bailey, speaking in existentially unruffled tones, offered many useful suggestions: Leave your phone in the other room when you need to get work done. Drink more caffeine. "We are what we pay attention to," he reminds us. Then he said something that surprised me: "Letting your attentional space overflow affects your memory."

Indeed, I soon discovered that this is a classic finding of

memory research, known for decades: distraction breeds forgetting. To say it another way, the way the neuroscientists say it, interrupting someone's attention by introducing a "secondary task" (responding to a text message, for example) means this person will not "encode" their present circumstance in all the rich, associative detail necessary for a memory to form and hang around awhile. Attention, it turns out, does not concern only our present circumstance. It bears directly on both our past and our future. What will fail to make it into my memory bank because I'm too busy scanning headlines and replying to text messages to pay attention to my life? And yet, even in the midst of that very train of thought, I go ahead and pull my phone out of my pocket, for no particular reason.

That's how it is. We have entered into a situation where the gadgets we carry around with us—and the cognitive rhythm they dictate—are pitted against the possibility of deep engagement, or thorough "encoding." They ask us to be anywhere but here, to live in any moment but now. What struck me was this: we treat such changes as inevitable, even while we lament them, seek antidotes and alternatives, enroll in meditation classes, digital detoxes, silent retreats. I wanted to understand why we choose to pixelate our own attention spans, then hungrily search for ways to patch ourselves back together.

I found that I was still asking such basic questions as: What do we mean when we talk about attention? Perhaps it was inevitable to ask such questions now, in our Silicon age, glued to our screens as we are, our attention in pieces, forever divided among the countless demands our devices ask of it. In any event, these were the questions I found myself asking, found myself stuck with. In the years after Adderall, these questions became the quest I embarked upon.

In the beginning, I did not see how desperately personal this whole thing really was. After all, what is the question of attention really about, if not this: What is worth paying attention to? Hanging on to? *What matters?*

One might think that on my quest to comprehend the elusive force we call attention, I would have turned without further delay to that subject's great philosopher king. William James, the nineteenth-century thinker, brother of the novelist Henry James, son of the theologian Henry James, Sr., godson of Ralph Waldo Emerson, wrote the seminal texts on attention that still, inevitably, garnish so much of the contemporary writing on the subject, despite being 130 years old.

It is true that I duly went to Amazon.com and ordered a copy of James's *The Principles of Psychology,* volume one, knowing full well his place in the attention literature, even regularly quoting fragments of his famous statements on the subject, such as "Everyone knows what attention is. It is the taking possession by the mind, in clear and vivid form, of one out of what seem several simultaneously possible objects or trains of thoughts . . ." Yet when the paperback version of his tome arrived at my door, I found myself unable even to open it.

At college, I might have swallowed a blue pill to attend to James's thoughts on attention. I was without those blue pills now, and worse, much worse, I was a citizen of the year 2017, with all of its base distractions. How could my brain really hope to tangle with William James when it had been so thoroughly retexturized by the frequency with which I checked Instagram? (What was I even looking for there?) Not to mention the headlines that now reached me of their own volition, arriving on the screen of my phone at an unpredictable rate, leading me to other headlines, other articles, which I couldn't even hope to finish, due to the urgent pull of fresh text messages and emails, or even the mere knowledge of the replies I owed, to say nothing of the instant messaging dispatches that often interrupted those emails, most of them typed by my brother somewhere in an office in Los Angeles.

By the time William James arrived on my stoop, therefore, it had become all too clear to me that my brain had not come through the Great Interruption unscathed. Apparently, it was no longer the relatively studious organ it had been with the pills, but really also without them, before them, back when I had not possessed an email address or had ever heard the name Mark Zuckerberg. And so my collection of William James sat on my desk, topped by a softback cover displaying his bearded countenance in sepia tones, alienating me even further from the realities of his day.

But I inched toward him, obliquely. Through biographies and essays, I began to rake in a miscellaneous collection of evocative details. I learned that as a young man, he'd had a nervous breakdown while traveling through Berlin, that his first book wasn't published until he was forty-nine years old, that he experimented with nitrous oxide, that his father had a wooden leg and wrote long, unappreciated theological tracts and tried to bully his son into a career in the sciences, though William himself had wanted to be an artist and had studied painting before giving up and going to Harvard Medical School. Intriguing details, all of them. And, as well, this observation: "One finds James when one needs him." So writes Jessa Crispin, in her book *The Dead Ladies Project*. And finally, I did. I needed him.

The first thing I discovered was that he understood, in his nineteenth-century way, my twenty-first-century plight. "Most people probably fall several times a day into a fit of something like this: The eyes are fixed on vacancy, the sounds of the world melt into confused unity, the attention is dispersed so that the whole body is felt, as it were, at once, and the foreground of consciousness is filled, if by anything, by a sort of solemn sense of surrender to the empty passing of time," James wrote. "Every moment we expect the spell to break, for we know no reason why it should continue. But it does continue, pulse after pulse, and we float with it, until—also without reason that we can discover—an energy is given, something—we know not what—enables us to gather ourselves together, we wink our eyes, we shake our heads, the background-ideas become effective, and the wheels of life go round again."

If this was not the most vivid and thorough description of my relationship to Instagram, I know not what could possibly be. The vacancy of my gaze and, more broadly, my mind as I passively surrendered to the scroll of images generated by other people's lives was exactly as James had said: a spell, one I could not comprehend, least of all when I was deep inside it. For the fact was, this particular kind of capture brought none of the upsides that I experienced when absorbed in reading and writing, or swept up in a great conversation, to say nothing of music, running, sex—all pursuits largely if not entirely unmediated by the young gazillionaires of Silicon Valley. Instead of aliveness, what I felt after such technology-induced spells was sad, inadequate, and, most of all, uninspired.

There are endless metaphors for attention, waxing and waning according to the moods of the day. Attention in the twentieth-century scientific research is, we often hear, a "spotlight" or "searchlight," whose beam we use to select one feature of our environment to focus on at a time. For James, and others of his era, a more compelling analogy came from water: James compared all mental activity itself to a "stream of thought" with attention as the single force capable of freezing the rushing tide. "Without selective interest," he wrote, "experience is an utter chaos."

It is worth emphasizing that the concept of selection has been a part of the attention conversation since the modern attention conversation began. Attention is by definition a trade-off. As the philosopher Émile Durkheim put it: "We are always to a certain extent in a state of distraction, since the attention, in concentrating the mind on a small number of objects, blinds it to a greater number of others." So that, then, is the rub, the ongoing predicament. What to choose?

When James arrived at Harvard's medical school in 1864, it was far from the elite institution it is today. In the 1860s, leeches were still on the curriculum, the cure for liver problems, the young doctors learned, when applied to the anus. Five years before James got to Harvard, Darwin had published *On the Origin of Species,* and his theory of evolution was the subject of a great deal of debate on both sides of the Atlantic. Before entering Harvard's medical school, James had apprenticed himself in the studio of William Morris Hunt, pursuing his first great love: painting. Later, perhaps thinking of his hours under Hunt's auspices, he would write, "It is only the great passions, which, tearing us away from the seductions of indolence, endow us with that continuity of attention to which alone superiority of mind is attached."

A kind of forced indolence was in fact often his fate: in his younger decades, especially, he was frequently unwell, as was his brother Henry. This was their great shared subject: their ailments. They sent each other endless letters across the Atlantic, Cambridge to Rome, William describing his dark moods and his faulty vision; Henry, his digestive woes. It wasn't until the

1870s, late in the decade, that James stabilized enough to make his real entrance on the intellectual scene with his much-read ideas on consciousness, will, and attention.

Attention was not a new idea, of course. Nor was it primarily a Western one. One could begin virtually anywhere, and at any point in time, telling the history of attention: as meditation, as prayer. But to me, one of the most intriguing stories was that of the tiny cult of European naturalists who popped up in the eighteenth century and became entranced with their own powers of attention. They studied bugs, but it was no mere nine-to-five pursuit. The historian Lorraine Daston has chronicled their efforts in *The Moral Authority of Nature:* Take Charles Bonnet, naturalist from Geneva, who spent twenty-one consecutive days, from 5:30 in the morning to 11:00 at night, staring at a single aphid. As the weeks passed, he began referring to it as "mon puceron," recording every painstaking detail in his journals. His French counterpart René Antoine Ferchault de Réaumur once spent fourteen hours counting the number of bees that left their hive. (Eighty-four thousand.)

Naturalists such as Bonnet justified their endless hours of attending to the wing of a fly or the guts of a worm with a kind of Aristotelian cry: "There be gods even here." After all, these too were creatures of God, reflections of God's "exquisite handiwork." These men believed that with the force of their attention they could bestow on lowly insects something like divine worth, redeem them from their repulsive irrelevance. Yet where they had embarked on a kind of holy mission of focus and attention, the very act of attending changed their relationship with the object of study. "Originally motivated by piety, unwavering attention directed to humble objects became an end in itself, infusing them with aesthetic and sentimental value," Daston writes. Bonnet was crushed when he lost track of his aphid one day. Réaumur, for his part, was so moved by the spectacle of the bees he'd been observing trying to save their half-drowned queen that he rewarded them with honey for their "good-intentions." "The naturalists came to regard their bees and aphids and even insects extracted from horses' dung with wonder and affection," Daston notes. As well, they derived enormous pleasure from the very act of paying close attention, noting that, absorbed in their observations, they could forget their own discomforts, their vertigo, their foot pain, the broiling summer heat.

Among themselves, the naturalists revered the ordealism of sitting for endless hours with probing eyes, but, within society at large, their behavior approached the taboo. "Too much attention paid to the wrong objects spoiled one for polite society as well as for the sober duties imposed by family, church and state," Daston explains. Satirists made fun of them. Conversation manuals warned of the terrible rudeness of "ostentatious learning."

Ever been stuck at a dinner table next to someone like this? I seem to remember an interminable conversation about "the cloud" in the early days of cloud computing. The narrator went on and on, schooling me on the baroque technicalities of remote data storage. Those seventeenth-century conversation manuals would have come in handy. He did not know it, but his faux pas linked him to the naturalists of yore. "The pathology of misdirected attention," Daston writes, "rendered its victims oblivious to the social cues of age, rank, sex, vocation and education that skilled conversationalists effortlessly registered and to which they adapted their themes and manner accordingly."

"Ultimately," she notes, "only God was a fitting object for such rapt attention."

It was toward the end of the nineteenth century that attention as a secular force, attention in its everyday, moment-to-moment forms, began gaining currency in scientific circles. Jonathan Crary, attention historian, documents its trajectory. Attention was emerging from the intellectual background to become the target of laboratory-dwelling researchers, who were trying to answer some of the most basic, concrete questions. Among the unknowns: How many things could we pay attention to simultaneously? Indeed: *Could* we pay attention to more than one thing at the same time? How did a person attend to some things and not others? Was attention voluntary or automatic? In his Leipzig lab—the first in the world to study human psychology experimentally—Wilhelm Wundt was busy measuring his subjects' reaction times to various stimuli he presented to them, trying to figure out what happens when the mind is confronted with two signals arriving at the same instant. Wundt was on a mission to make a science of self-reflection.

In his *Principles of Psychology,* William James reflected upon Wundt's studies, those precise, fine-grain, nuts-and-bolts pursuits, but, as well, he "complained about the tedium of German psychology, its immersion in monotonous details, and its failure to uncover even a single elementary law," according to one James biographer, Gerald Myers. In his own writing on attention, James elevated the subject to loftier heights, introducing a philosophical grandeur and a poetic sensibility to the inquiry. In considering what grabs our attention and what doesn't, James writes, "A faint tap per se is not an interesting sound; it may well escape being discriminated from the general rumour of the world. But when it is a signal, as that of a lover on the window-pane, it will hardly go unperceived."

The general rumour of the world . . . It is phrases like these that made James irresistible. Through the thicket of reaction-time charts and graphs to be found in his pages, and the toxic drumbeat of my own iPhone lying facedown across the room, luring me with its potential unseen messages, I read on. James separated involuntary attention—as when responding to an outside force too compelling to ignore—from the willed, as when concentrating, for example, on intellectual work with effort and determination. "No one can possibly attend continuously to an object that does not change," he wrote. "The *conditio sine qua non* of sustained attention to a given topic of thought is that we should roll it over and over incessantly and consider different aspects and relations of it in turn. Only in pathological states will a fixed and ever monotonously recurring idea possess the mind."

In James's treatment, attention was the means by which a person could claim agency and create a meaningful life. Attention, for James, was precious, essential, and often difficult. "My experience is what I agree to attend to," he famously wrote, but he never pretended that "agreeing to attend" was a simple and effortless act. Voluntary, purposeful attention in a world of constant distraction was difficult, even then. It is perhaps the most difficult of all the tasks that confront us. "Whether the attention come by grace of genius or by dint of will, the longer one does attend to a topic the more mastery of it one has," James wrote. "And the faculty of voluntarily bringing back a wandering attention, over and over again, is the very root of judgment, character, and will."

In his personal life, James took a fire-hose approach to attention. Whatever came at him, he embraced. He believed this was how it should be done. "There can be no real doubt that William James, in his heart of hearts, embraced and welcomed chaos, cataclysm, change, *Zerrissenheit,** impulse, and chance," writes Robert Richardson, a James biographer. "He required himself to meet every demand . . . James needed constant challenges and perpetual demands, if only to prove that the inner well hadn't run dry." James was often to be found on a ship heading to Europe, compelled to accept the many invitations to lecture that arrived at his door, likely to write the contributing chapter, to dine, to travel, to hike. His world perpetually expanded.

At sixty, James began an enthusiastic friendship with a new, like-minded correspondent, the French philosopher Henri Bergson, seventeen years his junior. Bergson and James shared a taste for the territory outside the strict rationalism of the scientific method: what might be called the mystical, or the occult. James, for his part, visited mediums and experimented with mescaline. He was interested in all of human behavior, all forms of human consciousness. Bergson too was unafraid to venture beyond the strict boundaries of science. He wrestled with the idea of attention and perception in his book *Matter and Memory,* writing that attention always proceeds on two different axes, the present and the past. Man was more than an automated response to his present surroundings—his memories were constantly in play, enriching his connection to the present. "The more I

* Torn to pieces–hood.

think about the question, the more I am convinced that life is from one end to the other a phenomenon of attention," Bergson wrote to James, just after the turn of the century.

The timing of all this was not a coincidence. James didn't just happen to take up the subject of attention when he did; neither did Bergson, Wundt, Théodule Ribot, Max Nordau, Edward B. Titchener, Henry Maudsley, or the rest of the thinkers engaged with the subject in the last years of the nineteenth century and the first of the twentieth. Jonathan Crary argues in his dense, erudite way that attention was thrust forward as a whole new kind of problem in these particular decades. It was the era of mass-scale industrialization, when workers were expected to stand in factories all day and somehow maintain perfect vigilance throughout. Indeed, their *inattention* could imperil the whole scheme. "Part of the cultural logic of capitalism demands that we accept as *natural* switching our attention rapidly from one thing to another," Crary writes in *Suspensions of Perception.* The sociologist Gabriel Tarde described the impositions of the "machinofacture" economy as ones that forced workers to "an exhaustion of attention [that] is a new subtler form of torture, unknown to the crude purgatories of earlier times."

And yet, if a capitalist economy had forced the shape of attention to change, what, exactly, was attention's native state? With no interfering environments, no factory assembly lines to monitor, no iPhones in our pockets, what would our natural attentional rhythms look like? In *The Shallows,* Nicholas Carr argues that human attention had gone through a drastic restructuring long before industrialization: with the invention of the book. "The natural state of the human brain, like that of the brains of most of our relatives in the animal kingdom, is one of distractedness," Carr writes. "To read a book was to practice an unnatural process of thought, one that demanded sustained, unbroken attention to a single, static object." The reshaping of human attention by literature was, in its way, as violent as the relentless churn of factory life, strange as it is to say.

"The problem of attention is essentially a modern problem," Titchener observed, shortly before the turn of the century. As more and more of these experimentalists and philosophers lent their minds to the problem of attention, it became clear, Crary writes, that attention was not the stable force it had formerly been understood to be, but rather volatile, entirely inseparable from the distraction that inevitably followed. "Attention always contained within itself the conditions for its own disintegration, it was haunted by the possibility of its own excess—which we all know so well whenever we try to look at or listen to any one thing for too long."

What's more, Crary points out, the newly urgent focus on attention brought an inherently destabilizing realization: if, as was now becoming clear, attention differed so dramatically from one person to the next, if we are each, indeed, constantly selecting a narrow slice from an infinity of options, then the illusion of one shared reality is shattered. And where and when could this be more obvious than here and now, as we move through our shared public spaces while visibly, flagrantly, consumed by the private realities playing out on our screens?

As so often happens in the history of science, a subject that is passionately taken up for a decade or two can gradually be put down again, evaporating from the forefront of inquiry when the vogue for thinking in the old way succumbs to the new. This is more or less what happened to attention. "The physiology of attention is still a dark continent," George Herbert Mead's seminal *Mind, Self, and Society* would note in 1934. Attention had faded from the central concerns of the day as the nineteenth century bled into the twentieth. In psychology, the behaviorists rose to power, stressing their radically simplified model of stimulus and response to explain human behavior. Attention—implying agency, implying individual variation—didn't even come into it. "The term 'attention' was effectively banished from the vocabulary of scientific psychology: the dominant theorists of the day found it useless," wrote Daniel Kahneman, future Nobel laureate, in his 1973 tome *Attention and Effort.* But the 1960s, and the rise of cognitive psychology, had brought attention back from the darkness. It was, once again, the question that so many were trying to answer. Indeed, the most basic, fundamental mysteries about the nature of attention remained. Perhaps the most fundamental of all: Can attention ever truly be divided? If we are having one conversation, are we also following the substance of a second? If we are driving and talking, are we lending our minds to both at once, or cycling back and forth between them?

Though William James had so famously promised "everyone knows what attention is," it turned out, a century and a half later, this really wasn't the case. There was even, I discovered, a term in use by academics to label the overstepping: "Jamesian confidence." I came across this phrase in a paper titled "There Is No Such Thing as Attention," a paper with a certain kind of renown in its field. According to its author, Britt Anderson of the University of Waterloo, we have lost our bearings in the quest to make headway into the central mysteries of attention. Anderson names a few central culprits, first and foremost researchers' tendency to "binarize," to claim that attention is either one thing or the other. "We try and shoehorn everything into being either this or that," he writes. For example, the question of "pre-attentive" versus "attentive" processing:

How much is the conscious act of paying attention actually preceded and made possible by a kind of unconscious, involuntary scan? A preparing for the act of paying attention? For a long time, Anderson says, these two acts were accepted as distinct, pre-attention preceding attention in crisp serial fashion. Many studies were conducted to support this point. "A million trials later we conclude that in fact there are not two distinct kinds of searches," Anderson notes.

Beyond the false binaries, attention research is muddied by "plurality": there are too many different meanings of the word, too many different references. There is visual attention, and auditory. There is local versus global spatial attention. There is attentiveness in the sense of being prepared, there is vigilance that can shade over to a pathological excess of attentiveness, and there is the opposite pathology, a deficit of attention. There is the mystery of the attention span. And so on and on. And on. "The fact that there are so many variable definitions empowers researchers to create newer, eclectic ones," Anderson argues. Anderson's overall point, though, is even more broad. Rather than thinking of attention as a specific, concrete force, capable of causing certain effects, we should think of the inverse: "attention" as a word for many different brain states that are themselves *caused* by different environments, different conditions. "We need the right terms if we are to say something meaningful."

All of which I was in the slow process of gathering, when I took my seat on a hard-backed chair in the elegant, light-filled faculty lounge of New College, Oxford. I still didn't know exactly what I was after, in this search for attention. Was I trying for intellectual understanding? For self-improvement? For some way to feel okay about the invasion of technology into our attentional fields? For someone to tell me that science said our phones have changed nothing? Or our phones have changed everything? For some way to accept my own shortcomings?

But there in Oxford, I had come to drink tea with Mark Stokes, the neuroscientist who heads Oxford's prestigious "Attention Group." Youngish, dark-haired, and Australian, Stokes, in white canvas sneakers, deftly consumed biscotti beneath an oil portrait of an unidentified Oxford luminary, a man who had once likely sat in this same faculty lounge himself. It was inevitable, I knew, that I would come face-to-face with neuroscience, the discipline currently in charge of setting the terms by which we humans seek to understand ourselves. My first question to Stokes was the one I most wanted to know the answer to: Has science convincingly defined "attention"?

"Certainly not," Stokes replied. "I think one of the difficulties is that 'attention' is a common term. It's a normal, everyday term that carries a lot of baggage. It's not a scientific term; it's something borrowed from normal language, which means that everyone who comes into the field comes with all that sort of folk psychology."

Though attention might be an idea that belongs to all of us, Stokes said, what so often occurs in laboratories devoted to studying attention is a scenario that many outside of science would not recognize as having much to do with the thing itself. For instance, the research paradigm now accepted as the gold standard requires subjects to sit in a contraption that doesn't allow them to move their eyes, as stimuli are presented in their peripheral vision. With this fixed eye position, researchers believe they can escape the "confounding" influence of eye movements on attention, isolating the relevant brain processes themselves.

"People agreed: the real science is looking at what happens when you *don't* move your eyes," Stokes said. "But of course then you end up in a weird situation. Because of course we *do* move our eyes, and that's important. We are not just a brain in a jar." Can this level of artifice—an essential part of precise, scientific reductionism—ever be relevant for those of us seeking to understand that multifaceted, waxing and waning, lived experience we know as attention?

"The jury is out," Stokes told me. "The field is so dominated by visual attention. It's important, but the lay idea of attention is really much more conceptual than that. You've got those classic quotes from William James, how attention is the 'bringing into mind in clear and vivid form,' and all this stuff, and that's really what people *think* of attention—it's focus, it's concentration—and that's really not been studied very much. You open a textbook on attention and it's all, like, looking at orientation patches in visual fields of fixated monkeys. Not what the average person on the street thinks about when they think about attention."

"Or cares about," I added, pointedly. "Especially in our era when we're living through the disintegration of attention."

"Why?" said Stokes.

I knew we were now wandering away from the thrust of the conversation: I had come here to ask Stokes about the state of attention science in general, and his lab's focus in particular. Not the more anecdotal, subjective, controversial, and all-around difficult-to-pin-down lived phenomenon of human attention in the age of Silicon Valley.

"Well, with the invasion of iPhones," I said.

"But again, that depends on what you mean by 'attention.' With the Internet, it's splintered concentration. You're attending *more*. It's not very sociable to sit at a dinner table attending to your phone, but informationally, it's actually richer. There's lots of attention going on, but it's just on the phone."

"But it's not sustained attention," I replied.

"Well, no, that's another aspect of attention that's different to the experimental notion of attention," he said. "Concentration is the strongest lay idea of attention that's not very well studied in our field. I think we do concentrate a lot now, it's just not on the right stuff."

"Yes, and we all know it feels wrong," I said, knowing how such a statement would sound to a hard scientist, trained to gather data, to think empirically, not to make such childish statements about how something "feels."

"Because we've got a higher goal in mind. We know we should be working on that book or whatever," Stokes said. "But in terms of computational neuroscience, it's all the same. There's nothing better about focusing on the book than there is on focusing on our phone."

Stokes told me, as if I couldn't already tell, that when it comes to technology, he's an optimist. Lucky him, I thought. What am I, exactly?

We said goodbye and I wandered back out onto the cobblestone, fairy-tale Oxford streets. I felt that my own brain had been powerfully affected by the technology I carried with me in my pocket at all times; I knew my relationship with literature had shifted, that my concentration had frayed, that my own sense of optimism on behalf of us all was never lower than when looking over to see that every person around me was squinting into their tiny screens. It was as if, with our eyes cast phoneward, we were all telling one another, all the time, "You— whoever you are—are no longer worth my real attention."

And yet, I couldn't walk for ten minutes through the magisterial Oxford streets without taking out my phone to consult my "Moves" app, which tracked my steps, to monitor incoming texts from back home in the States, and, of course, to engage in the life-draining blur of the infinite Instagram scroll. This was all to say nothing of our political situation: with the election of Donald Trump to the White House the year before, it had become in some real sense our civic duty to be all the more glued to our phones, assiduously tracing every new headline, every new tweet, so that we might—at the least—bear witness to what was happening to our institutions and values. Tuning out of the endless news cycle, turning away from our screeching screens, now bore the stigma of political complacency.

At home, an entire shelf of my bookcase creaked under the weight of doomsday literature, title after title concerning our age of distraction. I owned these books, but I read them slowly: I did not seem to have the attention to absorb thousands of pages on the death of attention. I told myself that any writer must know they risked boring their readers in railing against our technology-soaked lives. Life in the age of the iPhone was here to stay, was it not? As well: Who was to say that this technological revolution was fundamentally different, larger, or more significant than the great upheavals that organize history, the ones that bring change and wreak havoc? We've all heard the argument before: each such disruption, from the printing press forward, has provoked hand-wringing over the future of mankind. Has the Internet spawned a truly new breed of catastrophe?

And yet, wandering Oxford's ancient byways, the site of centuries of scholastic concentration, I came back to what I always came back to: the breathtaking *casualness* with which I had succumbed to the new habits and rhythms my phone asked of me.

The nonchalance with which I had given up deeper, sustained engagement in favor of perpetually splintered focus. And I knew it wasn't just me, of course. I wasn't the only one acting as if my ill-defined, ever-elusive, utterly precious attention didn't really matter at all.

6

"Attention."

It's the first word of Aldous Huxley's last novel.

"Attention."

It's the last word of Huxley's last novel. And, in some sense, it is Huxley's last word, his legacy. *Island,* published shortly before the great English novelist's death, lays out the themes, life's big ingredients, that Huxley was finally most engaged with.

Huxley had always intrigued me, but as a historical figure more than as a writer. His unusual life had taken him around the world: from the corridors of the elite English educational system to sunny Los Angeles, where he befriended Greta Garbo and Charlie Chaplin and pushed the boundaries of his consciousness with psychedelic drugs. Now embarked on my attention-minded quest, I found that the more I read of Huxley, the more preoccupied I became with the question of how he wound up at his final conclusion, his final prescription: attention. Attention always. "Attention to attention," as one of the Islanders advises.

Huxley is best known, of course, for *Brave New World,* the novel he published in 1932, his dystopian legend. Nearly a hundred years later, it is often cited as an early warning of our current predicament: our technology-love, our stupefied state, as we stare endlessly into our shiny screens. In Huxley's *Brave New World,* humanity has been engineered in a lab to be maximally productive, consumerist, and compliant. No one is ever left alone with their thoughts: at all times, there are crowds, activities, diversions. In fact, when one slightly rogue character, Bernard Marx, takes his date, Lenina, alone to the ocean, away from the usual diverting technologies and omnipresent crowds, she is repelled. "But it's horrible," she says. Huxley writes: "She was appalled by the rushing emptiness of the night, by the black foam-flecked water heaving beneath them, by the pale face of the moon, so haggard and distracted among the hastening clouds. 'Let's turn on the radio,'" she says. "'Quick!'"

Like everyone else around her, she is entirely unused to being with her own thoughts. She is, in fact, terrified of them. For her, for her fellow citizens, when thoughts threaten to bubble up, when unease creeps through the regularly scheduled program, there is soma. These are the tablets the population eagerly swallows down, the socially sanctioned pills that can whisk them for any length of time on a holiday from their own minds. "Was and will make me ill," Lenina intones, repeating the lines she has been fed all her life. "I take a gramme and only am."

In this brave new world, there is no literature, there is no Shakespeare. For one thing, it's too beautiful. "Beauty's attractive, and we don't want people to be attracted by old things," explains one character, an architect of the new social order. "We want them to like the new ones." And here, is it so far-fetched to recognize echoes of our own impulse to upgrade and update, to fetishize the constant novelty that only technology can provide? The one character who turns to the old, who inhales Shakespeare—the outsider they call The Savage—winds up dead by his own hand, swinging from a noose in the book's final scene.

Huxley's book is often regarded now, almost ninety years after its publication, as a premonition. It was as if Huxley were warning us that we were at risk of becoming so entranced by our own diversions, we would forget who we are, or, at least, who we used to be. From early in his adult life, Huxley was preoccupied by the question of man's relationship to technology. He never dropped the concern. Sybille Bedford, in her biography of Huxley, provides the transcripts of a 1961 interview Huxley gave on the BBC. In it, he remarked on a widespread sense that "man is now the victim of his own technology . . . instead of being in control of it." Huxley went on, "I think this is perhaps one of the major problems of our time. How do we make use of this thing? . . . We do have to start thinking how we can get control again of our own inventions. This is a kind of Frankenstein monster problem."

Huxley was born with the weight of family expectations already on his infant head. He came from not one, but two accomplished lineages: his grandfather was Thomas Henry Huxley, a biologist and major figure in advancing the theory of evolution (also said to have coined the term "agnostic," a defining sensibility for future Huxley boys). On his mother's side, his great-uncle was the poet Matthew Arnold. Aldous himself was recognized as different, special, *other,* by the time he was four or five. His temperament belonged to a higher plane. This quality in him was remarked upon by others all his life, wherever he went.

He had inner reserves that saw him through a painful childhood, rife with tragedy. When he was fourteen, his beloved mother died unexpectedly of cancer. Two years later, while he was a student at Eton, he developed an acute case of keratitis punctata and, almost overnight, lost most of his eyesight. He was forced to drop out of school and retreat to a bedroom in his father's new home in London. There, in his private darkness, he taught himself to read Braille and to play the piano.

I often think of this teenage Huxley, left alone to his own devices, motherless, his world in darkness, only his mind to rely on. Rather than fall to pieces, he became madly productive. Years later, he would write to a friend who had developed his own problems with vision about the coziness of reading Braille under the blanket. "Everything has its consolations," Huxley advised. I would always wonder about this period of near blindness in shaping Huxley's sense of what matters. Of what, ultimately, gets us through.

Growing up, Huxley had thought of becoming a scientist, as his brother Julian would be, but with his damaged eyesight, he wouldn't be able to use a microscope. A writer, then. To make money, he taught at Eton. His students misbehaved terribly at the back of his classroom, where he couldn't really see them. Huxley would look vaguely in their direction and occasionally say things like: "Oh! Do be quiet!"

One of these students was Eric Blair, the future George Orwell. I adored the great coincidence that would have these two men intersect in that high school classroom, both of them destined to write famous, dystopian novels. But in Orwell's version, *1984,* we do not lose ourselves to perpetual distraction, as Huxley imagined. Rather, we are conquered by the surveillance state. By 2020, of course, both writers would likely feel vindicated.

Huxley and his wife, Maria, were inseparable, codependent: she devoted herself to taking care of him, making up for his impaired eyesight by being his driver, by reading to him aloud for hours almost every night. She considered it incredible that a woman like herself, an "upstart little refugee" who could barely "spel," would have landed and kept "the prize of the artistic English world." According to Sybille Bedford's biography (Bedford was a close friend of the couple), Maria even helped arrange her husband's occasional affairs with other women, sending them autographed copies of her husband's books when the fling had run its course.

Together, the Huxleys lived as nomads, forever taking up and then abandoning residences, in Italy, in France, in England, then on to America, where they moved just before World War II. They landed on the West Coast, vacillating between the desert and Hollywood, where Aldous was hired to write a few different movies, earning income that often kept them afloat. Their longest-standing Los Angeles apartment was located at 740 North Kings Road, a fact that I discovered one day buried deep in Bedford's biography. Though the original house was long ago replaced by an apartment building, I still couldn't quite believe the coincidence: I had spent countless hours in the attached building next door at 750 North Kings Road, cooking dinner, watching the Oscars, crashing on the sofa. It was my brother's address for nearly five years.

As their life on the American West Coast went on, perhaps inevitably, Aldous and Maria gravitated more and more to the spiritual. Huxley began to study Vedantic Hinduism, attending an ashram in Hollywood shaped like the Taj Mahal, "surrounded by lemon trees and young girls meditating in saris."

Jay Stevens describes this essentially Hollyweird scene in his book on psychedelic history, *Storming Heaven*. Though Huxley was interested in meditation, he chafed at the need for a guru stipulated by the ashram. He was too much of an individualist.

Still, one could argue that Huxley had become every bit as much Californian as English by the time he embraced the belief system and practices known as "E Therapy." In a letter, Huxley explained: "There is a part of the subconscious non-self which is much less stupid than the self and personal subconscious, and can be relied upon to provide help if asked . . ." The quest, then, was for the "eternal consciousness," the E, the "deeper self." The prescribed approach, Huxley went on, was like meditation, but with an auditor present who asked you careful questions to guide you along. Aldous was told his E was quite "blocked," the road ahead a long one. Observing her husband's progress, Maria wrote in a letter, "Aldous's E functions chiefly in his work. But now, by developing it . . . It works more and more in everyday life . . . Now the treasure is flowing in torrents of gaiety and openness."

In his 1945 book *The Perennial Philosophy,* Huxley set out to synthesize the common ground among different mystical traditions. It was an abiding fascination, one that continued to grow the older he got. And it's no coincidence that just a few years after *The Perennial Philosophy* appeared, psychedelic drugs entered Huxley's life. In fact, he sought them out quite deliberately. The result would transform Huxley's own work and the future of psychedelic science in the West. Huxley wrote the blueprint for countless trips—and countless accounts of countless trips—to follow. It is still, to this day, a sacred text for many.

It was 1953 when Huxley sent a letter to Humphry Osmond, a young psychiatrist researching the effects of mescaline in a

Canadian hospital. Huxley didn't know it, of course, but the year marked the midpoint of what would prove a unique era in the history of psychedelic science. Since 1943, when a Swiss scientist named Albert Hofmann had first discovered the effects of lysergic acid diethylamide-25, the laboratory he worked for, Sandoz Labs, had been trying to figure out what to do with it. It was far from obvious. Made from the fungus that grows on rye, here was a substance that even in tiny doses produced incredible, colorful hallucinations, experiences like no other. But what was it good for? In psychiatry, doctors wondered whether LSD and mescaline, derived from peyote, could be used to model psychosis and schizophrenia. It might be possible, the thinking went, for psychiatrists to understand the cause of these mental disorders by replicating or approximating them on their own psychedelic trips.

Humphry Osmond was one of the doctors focused on this line of inquiry. When he received Huxley's admiring letter, he was intrigued by the novelist's proposition: Huxley, forever curious, wanted to try mescaline himself. Though they had not met, Osmond saw the potential immediately: maybe it would take not a scientist in a lab or a clinician in a hospital, but rather a novelist of Huxley's caliber to articulate and clarify the essence of these extraordinary substances. And so, with trepidation, he accepted an offer, extended by an equally nervous Aldous, to stay with the Huxleys at their home on Kings Road, bringing with him a small supply of crystallized mescaline.

It took Huxley one month to write his account of his first psychedelic experience. He named the slim book after William Blake's observation:

> *If the doors of perception were cleansed*
> *Everything will appear to man as it is, infinite.*

The Doors of Perception is my favorite of all of Huxley's many books. It is written with breathtaking simplicity and clarity. It is hard to convey the influence that Huxley's short text has had on every book about psychedelics that has followed. (And there are quite a number of them.) His descriptions and metaphors have informed the experience of generations of curious psychonauts, served as the road map to understanding what might be thought of as beyond understanding.

When Huxley swallowed the crystals of mescaline Osmond proffered, he was not beset with wild hallucinations or out-of-body experiences. He knew just where he was and what he was looking at. But the landscape had nonetheless shifted. Space and spatial arrangements no longer mattered. Neither did time: nothing, in fact, seemed less relevant. What struck him, what filled him with awe: "The books, for example, with which my study walls were lined. Like the flowers, they glowed, when I looked at them, with brighter colors, a profounder significance. Red books, like rubies; emerald books; books bound in white jade; books of agate; of aquamarine, of yellow topaz; lapis lazuli books whose color was so intense, so intrinsically meaningful, that they seemed to be on the point of leaving the shelves to thrust themselves more insistently on my attention."

Huxley echoed the philosopher C. D. Broad, writing that the brain is essentially "eliminative." It works like a reducing valve, "shutting out most of what we should otherwise perceive or remember at any moment, and leaving only that very small and special selection which is likely to be practically useful." In ordinary life, by necessity, our attentional field is so limited, so utilitarian, so heartbreakingly small. On mescaline, Huxley describes breaking through these constraints, to a global, even cosmic, attention, what he called "the Mind at Large."

"I looked down by chance, and went on passionately staring

by choice, at my own crossed legs. Those folds in the trousers—what a labyrinth of endlessly significant complexity! And the texture of the gray flannel—how rich, how deeply mysteriously sumptuous!"

This passage struck me hard, exemplifying the sensuality of Huxley's experience, the vivid way of seeing the world, as if from a child's perspective again, with an abundance of beauty and awe. Only later did I learn that Huxley wasn't actually wearing gray flannel pants while tripping on mescaline in West Hollywood. He wore blue jeans, but Maria made him change it in the manuscript, claims Sybille Bedford, wanting him more dressed up for the occasion. It's an unfortunate detail, but I offer it anyway.

Huxley's psychedelic book, revolutionary as it was, may not, in fact, have been his most controversial. After decades of living with partial or even near total blindness, Huxley had adopted a highly unconventional method by which, it was said, one could train oneself to see. It was called the Bates method, and Huxley's experience with it became the book he published under the title *The Art of Seeing*. In it, Huxley told the world that after implementing Bates's technique, he had restored his own vision and could now even read again, without glasses, whereas for so long he'd been dependent on Maria reading out loud to him in the evenings. When the book came out, doctors wrote irate letters to Huxley's publisher. I found one in the Huxley papers at UCLA.

"How an apparently sane person can write and cause to be printed for public consumption such absurd—nay, idiotic—material is a mystery to any scientifically disciplined mind." This outraged missive was dispatched by one Dr. Louis Smirnow, of Brooklyn, New York. I assume it was far from unique. But Huxley always maintained that he had gotten his vision back, that he'd successfully retrained his eyes. I couldn't help but think about this aspect of Huxley's life in metaphoric terms: he was forever refining his gaze, forever expanding what he could see.

Of course, there were blind spots. For example: he didn't know his wife was dying. Maria Huxley was so endlessly devoted to caring for her husband that she didn't tell him she was terminally ill until the last weeks of her life. She died at home in 1955, Aldous next to her, reading to her from *The Tibetan Book of the Dead* and telling her: "Go towards the light." In the last decade of his life, the decade following Maria's death, Huxley continued his experiments with psychedelics. He became publicly associated with the cause of psychedelic enlightenment.

One of those who questioned the validity of relying on drugs to wake up to higher awareness was the monk and influential author Thomas Merton. Merton wrote to Huxley, asking whether a drug, rather than contemplation alone, can lead to true enlightenment. Huxley wrote back a long description of what psychedelic drugs meant to him. First and foremost, Huxley told Merton, they fill him with "an unspeakable sense of gratitude for the privilege of being born into this universe . . . A transcendence of the fear of death. A sense of solidarity with the world and its spiritual principle . . . The experiences are transient of course; but the memory of them, and the inchoate revivals of them which tend to recur spontaneously or during meditation, continue to exercise a profound effect upon one's mind."

By now, Huxley's thought process had shifted markedly from where he'd begun as a young writer. From social satirist and cutting nihilist skewering the British elite, Huxley, in his later years, was often described as a visionary, a mystic. The marked evolution of his attention, of his basic point of orientation, was conspicuous and, in fact, a point of conversation among his readers. Thomas Merton would later write: "Everybody was talking about the way Huxley had changed. The chatter was all the more pleasant because of Huxley's agnostic old grandfather—and his biologist brother. Now the man was preaching mysticism."

In 1962, Huxley's house in Beachwood Canyon burned to the ground in a fire. Huxley lost many of his papers, his manuscripts, and his books. Right away, he requested a select list of replacements. From the American West Coast, Huxley's mind had gravitated East:

"Conze's Buddhism and his anthology of Buddhist texts. Suzuki's Zen Essays and Zen Doctrine of No-Mind, Evan Went's 3 books published by Oxford U. Press, Tibetan Book of the Dead, Milarepa, and Great Wisdom . . . Also Zimmer's Philosophy of India and Myths and Symbols of India. Krishnamurti's Commentaries on Living . . . And if anyone has a spare Dostoievsky or two, a spare War and Peace and Karenina and short stories of Tolstoy, a spare odd volume of Dickens, I shall be grateful to them."

Island, Huxley's last novel, takes place on the Island of Pala, a happy, enlightened society, spared a history of colonization due to its lack of a harbor. The Palinese know what matters, and, for when they forget, they have trained their birds to remind them. "Attention! Attention!" This is the island's constant background music. The birds know one other refrain: "Here and now, boys, here and now."

Into this mix, a dissolute English journalist named Will Farnaby washes up. From his sickbed, he immediately asks after the birds' refrain. "Why does he say those things?" Farnaby is answered by a patient Islander. "Well . . . That's what you always forget, isn't it? I mean, you forget to pay attention to what's happening."

Actually, Farnaby's main role in this novel is to be the recipient of lectures. A parade of Islanders come to his sickbed to monologue about the problems with the Western approach to life and the superiority of their own. Subjects include how to do everything from raise children to prepare for death, prevent illness, and have sex.

I wish I could say, for the sake of a clean narrative, that *Island* demonstrates how powerfully psychedelics can enhance creativity. That is the sort of story line we have come to expect by now, I suppose, as psychedelics once again promise to lead the way forward. Alas: in this case, the very opposite is closer to the truth. From the auspicious origins of *Brave New World,* the dystopian novel written with such elegance and wit at the beginning of his career, Huxley finished by presenting his Utopia novel: moralizing, bulky, and dull. For however much legitimacy there may be in the complaints raised by the people of Pala, page after page of self-aggrandizing lectures from smugly superior Islanders do not successful fiction make. Even Sybille Bedford, in her carefully loving biography, was forced to acknowledge the problems with the book. "To a great many . . . and this must be faced, the book was a boring tale of preaching goody-goodies," she wrote. "The attraction of Pala may well lie in the mind of the beholder."

But however mixed its response, the book enshrines Huxley's final theme: attention. Attention and love. This was his advice, his prescription, his legacy.

"It is never enough. Never enough. Never enough of beauty. Never enough of love. Never enough of life." These were some of his last remarks, looking at a perfect pink rose his second wife, Laura Archera Huxley, handed him as he lay on his death-bed in the Hollywood Hills. Laura Huxley captured these final moments in her own book, her memoir of her marriage to Aldous. It was November 1963. With the last of his strength, he dictated one final piece of work to her, a short essay on Shake-speare and religion. But as he grew weaker and weaker, hardly able to speak, Laura thought of the text that now meant so much to them both: *The Tibetan Book of the Dead.* "O Nobly Born! Let not thy mind be distracted." So exhorts the sacred text, address-ing the dying, instructing the dying on how to approach the final moment. They must "go on practicing the art of living even while they are dying. Knowing who in fact one is, being conscious of the universal and impersonal life that lives itself through each of us. That's the art of living, and that's what one can help the dying to go on practicing. To the very end." *Let not thy mind be distracted.*

It was perhaps in this spirit that Huxley, in a shaking hand, wrote on a sheet of paper his last request: to be injected with 100 micrograms of LSD. Laura complied, rising to retrieve the vial of LSD from the medicine cabinet. On her way to the bath-room, she noticed—and was horrified—that the other people in the house were glued to the television. How could they be watching TV while Aldous lay dying? Then she understood: JFK had been shot. She returned to her husband and injected him. He was dead a few hours later.

7

There was this idea of the American Dream . . . This was how the conversation began. I was on a boat, sailing past the dense nightlights of downtown San Francisco, heading toward the Golden Gate Bridge. The speaker was Dr. Stanislav Grof, well into his eighties, originally from Czechoslovakia but revered as a spiritual founder of the American psychedelic movement.

Grof, a psychiatrist, was in fact one of the people most closely associated with the first campaign—mounted more than fifty years ago—to bring psychedelic drugs, especially LSD, into mainstream life. Broad and solid, he was still handsome, unbowed by age, with a full head of dirty blond hair. Tonight, he was dressed for the chill in a blue windbreaker, his wife, Brigitte, hovering somewhere behind him, impatient to escort him onto the prow so that they could embrace as we passed beneath the bridge. But I didn't know that yet, so I continued asking Grof questions, scribbling down his oracular comments in my notebook as fast as I could. It was only much later, working through the archives at UCLA, that I would find an old Christmas card from Stan Grof, stashed away for posterity among Aldous Huxley's papers.

I had come to California on an assignment to write about the psychedelic research conference taking place in Oakland that week. All year, headlines had snaked through mainstream publications, describing the new craze in Silicon Valley that had tech workers swallowing tiny doses of LSD and magic mushrooms in the morning before heading off to work; veterans seeking treatment with MDMA to help their PTSD; clinics legally treating the depressed with ketamine. We were, it was becoming clear, living through a psychedelic renaissance. For the first time since the late 1960s, psychedelic science was back, poised to make not only social change but also, potentially, an enormous profit.

But I had an ulterior motive for coming west: I was trying to find out if the newly resurgent interest in psychedelic drugs had to do with our cultural shift away from one kind of attention. I had a suspicion, in other words, that a widespread craving to recover something we had lost, some way of being, was one of the reasons why psychedelics were beckoning so many new users, just at the moment when tech was saturating our lives.

I had spent ten years on one kind of drug, a darling of the pharmaceutical industry, but the only real insight it had given me was that I had to stop taking it. I was now drawn to the possibility that a different kind of drug altogether actually could offer a bridge to a profound new way of seeing the world. So here I was, sailing toward the Golden Gate Bridge in the darkness, a boatful of the psychedelic faithful huddled for warmth all around me.

The occasion for which we had gathered was the first meeting of the Multidisciplinary Association for Psychedelic Studies, or MAPS, to occur in four years. Thousands had turned up for the more than five days of presentations: this was the largest psychedelic research conference in the world, and MAPS the single most powerful player in advancing the psychedelic agenda. Scientists from schools like Johns Hopkins and NYU had come to present their research on such topics as using psilocybin (the active ingredient in magic mushrooms) to assuage end-of-life anxiety, to help deepen meditation practices, to search for the shared underpinnings of spiritual life, and—in a new study—to explore a possible cure for depression. The conference reflected the swelling interest and funding directed toward psychedelic drugs, more so now than at any time since LSD was first made illegal in the United States in 1966.

Grof himself was presenting the next day, talking about his many forays deep into the human unconscious. Grof had often played the role of goad, urging psychiatry ever deeper, to destinations that made many of his colleagues uncomfortable. For example, he argued that our psyches are indelibly shaped not only by our early childhood experiences, as has long been understood, but also by what happens to us in the womb, as well as during birth itself, a conclusion he reached during one of his early LSD trips. I didn't expect the opportunity to talk so closely that night to Grof, who was revered by the psychedelic community and thus rarely to be found alone. I had to ask him more, while I could.

"Why now?" I asked. "Why are psychedelic drugs seeing such an explosion of interest again?"

"The belief that you can make yourself happy by achieving something in the world: that view is getting dimmer and dimmer," Grof answered right away, in his soft, Czech tones.

Grof and his late wife, Christina, who died in 2014, coined a phrase to describe the state we are in. It is, they said, a "spiritual emergency," and nothing less. It is a spiritual emergency when we are motivated to forget that we are all interconnected, to one another, and to the natural environment we occupy.

"We're not going to make it if we keep doing what we're doing," Grof told me.

It was my impression that a great number of the people on that boat, not to mention the thousands who had gathered in Oakland for the week, shared this particular outlook.

At the time that I stood on that boat with Dr. Grof, I didn't know much about Aldous Huxley, or the world of psychedelics at all. I was at the very beginning of the search. What I knew, I knew primarily from two sources. The first and most powerful: long conversations with my old boyfriend David, whom I had lived with on Ninth Street during the Adderall years. Since then, he had gravitated more and more toward psychedelic experiences, attending dozens of ceremonies in places such as Topanga Canyon, Los Angeles; or Williamsburg, Brooklyn; Mexico and Peru. He was struggling to make money but laughed morbidly that even when he was broke, he would charge ayahuasca ceremonies on his credit card. He was actively remaking himself. We would meet for dinner every few months and he'd tell me all about what he was going through. I still regarded it all as fundamentally alien, these conversations about Amazonian jungle teas and shamans, intergenerational trauma revealed through plant spirits. But I could, in fact, see it for myself: David was filled with a new kind of insight, and, more strikingly, a new kind of peace. In fact, we were much closer now than we'd ever been as a couple.

The second source of information that had propelled me to Oakland was an article Michael Pollan had written in *The*

New Yorker a few years before. In it, Pollan reported on the new vanguard of psychedelic science: the research going on at Johns Hopkins and NYU, treating end-of-life patients with powerful, psychedelic trips. Pollan described how these patients, ravaged by cancer, facing death, emerged from even a single psilocybin experience with a newfound peace, a radical new perspective on their own place in the order of things. It was an astonishing piece of writing, and it spoke to one of the questions that mattered most to me, that moved me more than any other: the possibility, or, rather, the near certainty, that the way we are living our lives is simply not quite right. The possibility that there might be another way out of, or through, our modern predicament. And that it wasn't so far away, this alternative route. Indeed, it was already inside of us, dormant, waiting to be woken up.

From the San Francisco airport, on the BART train across the bay, I asked directions from a handsome young blond, an undergrad at Berkeley. I was curious to know if he'd heard about the conference that was starting the next day in Oakland, all about psychedelics. "Oh, is it connected to Bicycle Day?" he asked. "Bicycle Day?" I looked at him blankly. "Yes, the day Albert Hofmann discovered LSD. April nineteenth. Today." He went on to explain: this was the day, in 1943, when Albert Hofmann, the scientist at Sandoz Labs, had decided to ingest one of his experimental strands.

It was on his bicycle ride home, beset with colorful hallucinations, that Hofmann realized that this compound, lysergic acid diethylamide-25, was not like the rest. Hence: Bicycle Day, the birthday of LSD, which came into the world as World War II raged through Europe. I'd been schooled by a twenty-year-old who knew more about my current beat than I did. Perhaps an East Coast blind spot, then. It would prove to be the first of many: I was about to be introduced to a community dense with codes and signals, one with a kind of password, a question forever in the subtext: *Are you one of us?*

It started first thing the next morning, when I wheeled my suitcase into the Oakland Marriott to join the throngs buzzing through the cavernous conference rooms. The crowd was striking: all around me middle-aged academics in blazers mixed with the rainbow-haired, occasionally barefoot demographic more typically associated with such events as Burning Man and Coachella, which was taking place that same weekend, approximately five hundred miles south in the California desert. And yet this event too, it was clear, though composed of sober speeches and PowerPoint presentations, had the same raucous, joyful spirit of a like-minded community seeking refuge within itself, taking a much-needed break from the outside world, from the people who did not yet understand.

I wondered whether Michael Pollan himself was somewhere in these crowds, walking around with his own reporter's tools, gathering his own impressions of the colorful crowd. I had heard he was writing a magnum opus on psychedelics, and I looked for his familiar face, his thoughtful smile and wireframe glasses, in the welcome reception. I didn't see him there; nor was I able to secure one last cup of coffee. Instead, I made my way to the twenty-first floor to claim a seat at the workshop I'd signed up for, on the history and culture of psychedelics. Right away, I was drawn to a young woman in purple silk pants and a multicolored head scarf, doing yoga poses against the window, a panoramic view of downtown Oakland behind her. She was from Boulder, Colorado, she told me. With one leg still in the air, she told me that she was a psychotherapist who treats her patients with MDMA—also known as Ecstasy—part of the burgeoning underground of clinicians who do the same.

"Aren't you afraid you'll be caught?" I asked.

"It's my ethical duty to help clients in the highest way I can—so there's a protection around that," she said. "That's how my mentor talks about it."

She was on the vanguard of a movement that was still illegal, but perhaps not for much longer. MAPS's foremost campaign was devoted to getting the Federal Drug Administration's approval for the therapeutic use of MDMA for patients with PTSD. This was no longer a distant dream: research, already promising, would enter Phase 3 trials later that year, the final phase on any medication's journey through the FDA. By then, MAPS would have raised more than $50 million to do the science themselves.

"People who have been in talk therapy for forty years suddenly see results with one session of MDMA," she was telling me.

"And you're not afraid? Even though you are telling all this to the reporter in the room?" I asked her, gesturing again to my media badge.

"This feels like a safe space," she said.

Indeed, I would encounter a surprising lack of reticence from the people I spoke to over the course of the next five days. I was repeatedly offered drugs, even after I had mentioned the publication for which I was reporting. It was as if the drugs themselves offered a talismanic protection, and under their care, nobody could be exposed to harm or persecution. Everywhere I went, people sought me out in order to express their love for and faith in the power of psychedelics.

What we were waiting in line for was the evening entertainment, an event billed as the "comedy banquet." Once inside the enormous ballroom, I spotted a seat next to an attractive young couple, dressed up for the occasion, the guy in beard and black suit, and his beautiful girlfriend in a short black dress and fishnet tights. Almost as soon as I'd introduced myself, the man turned to me. "I'm really, really worried about how you're going to cover this conference," he said. His breath was powerful. I inhaled carefully. Exhaled.

"Interesting. What are you worried about?" I asked him. I was trying hard for compassion after a long reporting day.

"That you'll do what the media always does and focus on the druggies and hippies and make it seem like this is all about partying, when for some of us, these drugs are life or death," he said.

"Life or death? How so?" I asked. Tears began running down his face as he explained that he had PTSD from an abusive childhood and the only thing that allowed him to function at all was his regular use of ayahuasca, the powerful tea made from Amazonian tree vines. He excused himself and left for the bathroom. His girlfriend slid into the seat next to me. "He'll be okay," she said. "You have to understand it's so hard for him to even talk to someone like you, who went to college, and who could even think about his PTSD from anything like an intellectualized place."

I slipped away before dessert, but I was grateful for the encounter. It had underlined in the most visceral terms the extent to which these substances had transcended their 1960s Haight-Ashbury, "turn on, tune in, and drop out" origins to become a way of life that for many is nothing less than crucial— "life or death"—when there are few great options in Western medicine that reliably help most people with mental illness, and do so with tolerable side effects. For many, big pharma has not panned out.

And this is the point: the extent of suffering and illness in our rich, modern society was exactly why the proceedings could not be dismissed as 1960s-style excess, or the fantasies of a drugged-out community. If anything, the presence of Donald Trump in the White House, and the ever-present crackle of mania emanating from his Twitter feed, so profoundly interrupting our country's sense of itself, had the effect of further casting the psychedelic campaign in an utterly reasonable light. Against the backdrop of our current moment and its constant, crisis-like pitch, why not revisit—now with gold-standard science—the substances that had reorganized and revolutionized so many lives? It's easy to wonder: What do we, in fact, have to lose?

"Attention is concentration. That is where I think we became skilled—using a psychedelic and then *concentrating* on it," Amanda Feilding was telling me from across a conference room table. "I liked to be at that sweet point where I had more energy, more inspiration, but at the same time, I was in control of directing the attention so one could make use of it."

Feilding, also known as the Countess of Wemyss and March, is a British eccentric par excellence, prone to being photographed with a bird on her shoulder, head swathed in elaborate head scarves and turbans. Now in her seventies, she was dressed in her signature shade of emerald green, recounting for me her early years of research into psychedelic substances. Feilding had spent her life experimenting with them, first and mainly with LSD, starting in the 1960s, with which she began to make a kind of scientific study of her own acid trips, wanting to explore where she could go with her own creativity and concentration, and what might be the neural underpinnings for its powerful effect. She was an avid player of Go, which is considered the most elaborate board game in the world, with the largest possible number of moves. She began to discover that just the right amount of LSD, neither too much nor too little, gave her the winning advantage over her Go opponent, if he or she had not taken the drug.

Feilding's partner in this early research was a Dutchman, an amateur scientist, named Bart Huges; together, they advanced the idea that LSD redirects blood flow away from the domineering ego, toward more unconscious realms of the mind. These days, fifty years later, what Feilding referred to as "the ego" is approximately known in neuroscience as "the default mode network." It was, circa 2017, one of the most omnipresent phrases emerging from neuroscience labs, the official-sounding terminology for the brain regions that are active when we are not specifically occupied by any one task or another, the patterns of activity our brains fall back on when we are daydreaming, or ruminating, when we are blankly staring into space on the subway, not responding or reacting to anything in particular. These are the patterns of activities our brains resort to, in some sense setting the baseline tone of our lives.

But in the 1960s, Feilding had no such default mode network to contend with, only the Freudian language that was then still in vogue. Gradually, she expanded her repertoire, her battle to stretch beyond the censoring dictates of the ego. In fact, it's difficult to talk about Feilding without mentioning that in 1970, she drilled a hole in her own skull, a procedure known as trepanation, which some believe is a means to achieving an expansion of consciousness. One can, if one is curious, find a video on the Internet of Feilding performing this operation on herself, with no apparent physical pain. On the contrary, she appears to be in exceedingly good cheer as the blood runs down her face. I would add here that the hole is not visible beneath the hair, and that the woman herself doesn't appear to have lost a single ounce of earth-bound ambition through her extra orifice.

Feilding, nearly fifty years later, is still driven by precisely the same motivation as carried her through her youth: to wear down society's "taboo" on psychedelics. She spread out on the conference table between us glossy images made in brain labs: the fruits of the research that the Beckley Foundation, which she founded and had helped support, in collaboration with Imperial College London, among other schools. One showed a comparison between brain activity on LSD and brain activity without. Blurry trails of neon orange coat almost the whole of the LSD brain, demonstrating the increase in "connectivity" that occurs on the drug, allowing neurons to communicate with one another that would not otherwise confer. This, Feilding argued, might explain why LSD is said to open up whole new channels of thought and inquiry, allowing users to break out of stale patterns and discover, in some cases, enormous creative insight and innovation. In another photograph, Feilding pointed out a cluster of glowing, neon specks: they were brand-new brain cells that seemed to spring up the morning after an ayahuasca session, "neurogenesis," to use that vaguely biblical term. If true, the implication was significant: ayahuasca as a means to a new kind of mind, not the old, stuck-in-its-ways one you'd gone through your whole life with. But she was perhaps most excited about a new study she planned to launch at the end of the year, returning to her roots: the game of Go. She would test the effect of tiny doses of LSD on players' performance at Go, the ultimate test, she argued, of creative concentration.

"We have to reintegrate these compounds into society—and in order to do that, we have to use the very best science," Feilding was saying. "I never think that psychedelics are for everyone. But they *can* be very usefully used. I'm sure you know that William James was one of the first to express it. He said our daily consciousness is just a *trickle* and it's separated from a much wider consciousness through the filmiest of screens . . ." She mentioned that William James was friends with her grandparents. That, in fact, it was said that Henry James had based *The Portrait of a Lady* on her fierce, independent-minded grandmother Clotilde Brewster. I smiled when I heard William James's name spoken aloud in that conference room. I understood by then that James was the golden thread that would eventually run through all my best conversations about attention.

I suppose this is as good a place as any to mention that at that point in time, I had had little exposure to psychedelics myself. But not none. The first time I took magic mushrooms, I was in Central Park. I was twenty years old. I lay in the grass, staring up at my college boyfriend who had climbed into the tree above me. We stayed that way for hours, lost in our own thoughts, together. I came to a kind of epiphany that day: you don't need to worry now about your various ambitions. Just live. Those words rushed through my mind, unbidden. I hadn't even known how much worry I had spent on the question, until the apparent answer appeared to me. I never quite internalized them, I don't think, but I had never forgotten them. So it was not the case that I had no idea what everyone was talking about. But, a decade-plus later, I tended to shy away from full-blown participant status, even as those drugs or, to use the terminology, the "plant medicines," seemed to be everywhere, preferring instead to listen to other people's stories. I was too frightened to actually do something such as ayahuasca myself, to vomit for hours, to endure a narcissistic shaman convinced of his own divinity (I cynically imagined), to be trapped all night in the group dynamic, to encounter god knows what unconscious material, and then—and this was the real fear—to be the one person who didn't seem quite able to make it back to terra firma.

Yet I was magnetized by the ideas emanating from the new psychedelic science, sensing, like those around me this week in Oakland, the fundamental wrongness pervading so many aspects of our culture, of our habits and our selves. I wanted to throw off my own distractedness, self-obsession, and frivolity. I wanted to carry out my days purposefully, rather than disappearing into meaningless hours of Internet nothingness. Yet I couldn't help but notice that I resisted anything that threatened to really change me.

"You've had psychedelics?"

It was one of the first questions James Fadiman, the psychologist and writer, asked me as we sat across from each other at a restaurant near the Oakland Marriott. We had escaped for an hour so I could interview him about microdosing—the practice of taking a fraction of the typical dose of psychedelics, so small you don't experience any of the classic features of a psychedelic trip, just the faintest stirrings of a kind of vibrancy and well-being.

Fadiman studied my face. "Okay, good. Because honestly this wouldn't work. When I work with journalists who really have *no* experience, it's too tricky. Imagine if only one of us knew something about sex, and I talked about things I like to do to women . . ." Fadiman was grinning at me impishly. He was well into his seventies, but with the air of a much younger man, or one who doesn't defer to concepts like age. Everywhere he went, conference attendees swarmed him, wanting to discuss his microdosing project. Like Amanda Feilding, Fadiman was a member of the psychedelic old guard. He swallowed his first psilocybin capsule on a street corner in Paris in the early 1960s. It was given to him by Richard Alpert, now known as the spiritual leader Ram Dass, who had been his professor at Harvard. Within a few years, Fadiman had wound his way into the burgeoning psychedelic research occurring in Menlo Park, California, around Stanford University.

Fadiman, who had returned from Paris to get his PhD in psychology at Stanford, was in the middle of running a three-day off-campus study on LSD and problem solving when a letter arrived from the United States government declaring acid illegal in California. The famous story has it that, having read the contents, he looked up and announced: "I think we got this letter *tomorrow.*" Researchers and subjects finished out the day, wrapping up the study. It was the last one they would be able to do without breaking the law.

Fadiman now faced the altered landscape of prohibition. Though he was reasonably close to Ken Kesey and Tim Leary and other players in the world of renegade psychedelic research, he found he didn't desire to join his fate to theirs. "I wasn't an outlaw," he told me. "I couldn't handle those hours." Instead, for the next four decades, he went straight, patching together a career of other things: teaching in the Stanford engineering department, consulting, writing a psychology textbook.

"Did it bother you that you weren't doing what you really felt you were meant to be doing?" I asked him.

"Not in a profound depressed sense," he said. "It's a little bit as if you always wanted to move to California. But life's kind of interesting and New York has a lot of special things and then when it all breaks down you think *I hate it here* and you listen to 'California Dreamin''"—but on the whole you manage."

At seventy-four, Fadiman was back in the center of things, the man most closely associated with the wild popularity of microdosing. The practice of taking tiny, sub-hallucinatory doses of psychedelics is now the subject of countless articles and Internet videos, all touting the boost to productivity and creativity that such doses of mushrooms and LSD can bestow. Silicon Valley executives (with pseudonyms) regularly tell reporters about the upsides of their new socially acceptable psychedelic regime. Thousands are turning to psychedelics, particularly in microdose form, ironically enough to enhance their performance at work, burnish their professional gold stars, increase their productivity, and earn more money.

For the last several years, Fadiman had been asking that "citizen scientists" write to him with detailed descriptions of following "the Fadiman protocol" for their microdosing regime: one day on, two days off. He told me he had more than a thousand such reports, and that people see improvements in energy, mood, intellectual clarity, headaches, even menstrual cramps. Yet what most interested me in what Fadiman described was the robust improvement that people described when it came to their ability to pay attention. Attention—or, rather, distraction—was the second most common reason provided by Fadiman's citizen scientists for their decision to microdose, second only to depression. In fact, Fadiman told me, there might never have been a market for Ritalin had Sandoz Labs been able to study the benefits of microdosing.

"If you're one of these people—and many of us are—you have a list of what you want to get done. And certain items keep moving. Each day they move onto the new list. And you don't get to them. And if you look at that carefully, what you'll notice is there is some emotional issue around that," he said. "Procrastination is our way of avoiding putting attention on a topic. One of the reports we get on microdosing is that people are not procrastinating. When they have an item that comes up on their list, they are not caught up in the distractions from attention. They simply move ahead and do it."

"Why do you think?" I asked.

"They're able to not get caught up in their own extraneous thought loops, if I can create a totally nontechnical term. They have a heightened ability to focus their attention where they wish—and keep it there."

Fadiman told me he had almost run out of interest in the exacting, placebo-controlled scientific studies that must be done to carry microdosing to the next level of knowledge. Wherever he goes now, he runs into graduate students eager to play that role, to carry forward what he has only just picked back up, the legacy of all that was left unfinished when the 1960s came to a close and Richard Nixon moved into the White House and declared LSD a Schedule I substance. The group here in Oakland, under the auspices of MAPS, is conscious of all the strategic mistakes that were made in the sixties, all the trouble and disruptiveness that accrued around figures such as Ken Kesey and Tim Leary, practically guaranteeing government intervention. Now, many of the leading psychedelic advocates are not interested in conducting themselves like outlaws.

The director of MAPS, Rick Doblin, a sincere sixtysomething with a PhD from Harvard's Kennedy School, walked around the Marriott in a suit and tie. Doblin's life since 1986 has been devoted to the effort to push psychedelics back into legal use and mainstream life. It was his singular focus, his raison d'être, and yet, despite the decades he'd spent on the campaign, long stretches of time with no progress, he remained the eternal optimist. He greeted everyone with the same warm smile and with a palpable readiness to engage with them as deeply as they would like him to.

"We are not the counterculture," he repeatedly intoned that week. "We are the *culture*." It had become his mantra. Doblin was devoting the majority of his resources to MDMA, in part because he believed that MDMA didn't have the cultural baggage of LSD, with its anti-war, anti-government trappings, left over from the sixties. He had found that administering Ecstasy to people suffering from trauma, including dozens of veterans, allowed access to the most difficult, even intolerable memories, bypassing the searing pain to be able to look at the experience anew, to contend with it, reframe it, begin to weave it back into the story of one's life.

When I met him in his hotel suite, Doblin made his points to me with laser-focused urgency, sitting on the sofa across from me. "This is a time of incredible peril for the human species and for the health of the planet," he said, the late-afternoon sun streaming in through the window. "There's this sense of crisis, and at the same time, the recognition that the solution is going to be spiritual and psychological, rather than material."

When psychedelics first came on the scene in the fifties, Doblin argues, American culture wasn't ready for them. It was taboo to talk about death; hospice was a radical idea. Even yoga was viewed suspiciously, "as if sitting in the lotus position meant you were no longer a Christian." Now, the culture has shifted, and so too has psychedelic strategy. Doblin wanted to emphasize that his life's work "is not for the hippies, it's not for the crazies out in California. This is for the red states, this is for people facing 'despair deaths.' This is *for* the mainstream."

The days began to blur into one another, until it was Saturday afternoon, and I was sitting cross-legged on the carpet of the Marriott's grand ballroom with the rest of the overflow crowd. We were jammed together to listen to the slim, slight man onstage, who spoke with quiet intensity in a charmingly hybrid Hungarian-Canadian accent. This was Gabor Maté, a physician based in Vancouver, an expert in addiction, and an authority on the subject of how our culture at large had begun to fray. In fact, this was the subject of his talk today.

I got out my notebook and my tape recorder and settled in. Three years before, I had seen Maté's name somewhere—in a table of contents? On a conference program?—and it had pulled me to it as if it glowed on the page. I had sensed then that I would encounter him, or, rather, that I would seek him out and write about him, even though, at that time, I barely knew anything about him at all. A cursory Google search had revealed a very public persona, a man in his sixties, at least, with olive skin and melancholy eyes, often to be found on stages, in front of cameras, talking about trauma.

"Ten years ago, close to the end of my clinical work as a physician, if you told me I'd be addressing hundreds of people at a psychedelic conference, I wouldn't have known what drugs you were taking," Maté began now. "If we look at the society we live in, I'm speaking of the United States, which uses up a huge proportion of the world's resources and is ever hungry for more, so in this resource-splurging, incredibly wealthy culture, we have fifty percent of the adult population with chronic illness, seventy percent of adults are on some kind of medication . . . If in a laboratory we were growing microorganisms and if fifty to seventy percent of them were ill, what would you call that culture? We live in a toxic culture. We live in a culture that makes people sick."

Maté told us that in the past ten years of his life, he had come to understand that in the context of this toxic society, psychedelics were a powerful tool, perhaps the most powerful, for reconnecting with oneself, which is the essence of moving past trauma. *Trauma.* There it was again. I would soon understand that "trauma" was the word that defines Maté's work, his worldview, the dark pain, the scar tissue, that he is forever probing to find.

"Two years ago at the tender age of seventy-one, I participated in a psilocybin experience in San Francisco," he continued. "I was lying on the mat and the woman I was working with was sitting beside me, and all of a sudden I just started sobbing. I saw her, I was present as an adult, I knew I was in San Francisco, I knew that I was having a plant experience and I knew that this woman was a healer, but at the same time, I was a six-month-old infant and she was my mother. So two aspects were present: my deepest emotional childhood memories and my awareness as an adult. And I said to her words that I'm sure I would have wanted to say to my mother at six months of age as a Jewish infant of the Nazi occupation of Budapest, when our life was under threat almost daily, and the words that came out of my mouth, articulated to this therapist, were: *I'm sorry for having made your life so difficult.*"

When his speech was over, Maté welcomed questions at the mic. A woman with long dark hair, in a shiny red 1950s-style jacket and big black sunglasses, approached.

"As an indigenous person, even standing here, my heart is pounding in my chest like a jackrabbit because what I want to say is not necessarily going to make anybody happy," she began.

"What I want to say is that cultural appropriation is a form of re-traumatization to indigenous people." Her voice shook as it hit the upper registers.

She wanted, she said, for Maté to speak to the issue of "cultural appropriation" when it came to using plants such as aya-huasca or peyote, increasingly sought out by affluent white Americans and Europeans, who travel to foreign countries to take part in ancient healing traditions not their own.

"Listen, I get it, if that's what you heard me say, I can see why it would break your heart. I totally understand," Maté said. He went on. "Here's what I'm noticing from you right now: you're speaking from a deep wound. But I cannot stand here and heal your wound."

"That's not what I'm asking for," the woman replied, growing visibly more upset. She turned at that point to face the sizable audience. "I'm asking for everyone here to just be accountable for *your own white privilege.*" These last words she shouted while gesticulating toward us with one hand. We sat there, in our overwhelming whiteness, in our uncomfortable, riveted silence, as she crossed the ballroom and pushed out through the doors. Soon after, Maté took his own leave, rushing, he explained, to catch the flight to his next gig.

When I returned to New York, I spent the next week trying to track Maté down on the phone. I did not realize how difficult this task would be: he was, it seemed, forever on the move, off to his next conference, his next meeting, his next keynote address. Finally, I reached him one Sunday afternoon at his home in Vancouver. I wanted to interview him for a short article I was writing. I told Maté that my piece was about psychedelics, but that I was also working on a book where I hoped to expand these ideas. "A book about psychedelics?" he asked.

"No, about attention," I said.

"You do know I wrote a whole book about attention deficit disorder?" he asked.

"Yes," I said. "It's one of the reasons I so much wanted to talk to you."

This was April. I ask myself if I knew then, on some level, that eventually I would follow Maté to Central America, that soon enough, in his company, I would find myself on a mattress surrounded by people throwing up in plastic buckets. Did I know that then? Yes. I think I did.

8

I was back in San Francisco within the year. I'd returned in pursuit of a subject about which I had far more ambivalence than psychedelic science. I was making the trip that someone inevitably makes if they're trying to understand the current landscape of attention: I'd come to try to glimpse Silicon Valley for myself, the very infrastructure of our attention economy. But I landed at SFO with some sense of futility. I was here to try to gain some insight of my own into a land so mythologized and satirized, I wasn't even sure where, strictly speaking, it was located.

The attention economy itself, of course, is nothing new. We've long since existed within it. Tim Wu, the Columbia University law professor and writer, describes its evolution in his book *The Attention Merchants*. Wu points to an example we'd now consider charming or even quaint: the posters designed in the nineteenth century by the French artist Jules Chéret. All over Paris, these posters went up, displaying images of comely women showing lots of leg, advertising for wine, for the opera, for the music hall. In Paris, advertisements themselves were nothing new, but Chéret's vivid style—and all that naked female skin—was a radical innovation.

At first, Chéret was much admired for his posters, even awarded the Legion of Honor. But soon, his work had spawned imitators, unleashing a "poster craze" on Europe and America. Paris, the epicenter, became "hardly more than an immense wall of posters scattered from the chimneys down to sidewalks with clusters of squares of paper of all colors and formats . . ." goes one contemporary account.

It didn't take long for Parisians to demand the return of their beautiful city, with their sight lines uncluttered, their minds unmolested by more and more flyers urging them to spend money whenever they turned their heads. The municipal authorities took action, restricting the posters' placement throughout the city. Those restrictions remain in place today.

Across the Atlantic, at least a few Americans felt a similarly allergic reaction when, in 1948, the city of Washington, DC, struck a deal with Muzak. Background music and commercials began pumping into the city's trolleys and buses. Most DC commuters did not seem to mind the new noise level, but two lawyers felt differently. Franklin Pollak and Guy Martin sued the city, deeply offended by Muzak's invasion of public air space. Pollak and Martin were arguing against what they said amounted to no less than "an unlawful deprivation of liberty under the Constitution," writes Louis Menand in his description of the episode. By 1952, their case made its way to the Supreme Court. They lost, but exactly one justice agreed with them. William O. Douglas believed that this case was, at its core, about privacy, or "the right to be let alone," as he put it.

"The right of privacy," Douglas wrote in his dissent, "is a powerful deterrent to any one who would control men's minds." Douglas's opinion was duly recorded. And the Muzak played on.

We know from these episodes and others that it is possible, even logical, for human beings to experience the invasion of our attentional fields as viscerally as a punch to the gut. But from the beginning, it seems to me, we've let Silicon Valley and its obsession with advancing its own technologies steamroll us into a kind of stunned complacency. We flock to use the new platforms; we hang on Apple's every product launch; we revere famous technologists as modern gods. We fork over unimaginably personal details to entities whose actual intentions we cannot know. I once found myself at a "KeyMe" kiosk in a Bed Bath & Beyond, so intrigued by the machine's ability to duplicate my house keys on the spot that I cheerfully followed along the instructions that appeared on the screen: to upload my thumbprint into the ether. Suddenly, horrified, I yanked my thumb off the scanner, just short of the complete print. I called the customer service hotline and demanded: "Do most people just turn over their fingerprints, no questions asked, even if they've never heard of your company?" Yes, the woman explained; in fact, they are happy to, as they believe it makes their computerized key more secure. I begged her to erase whatever data they had on me. I have no idea whether she honored my request.

One hundred fifty times a day. That is how often the average American millennial checks her phone, according to one much-discussed study, commissioned by Nokia. And that was in 2013. We know from a robust and growing literature that every interruption can derail us from our original task for, on average, twenty-three minutes. What's one hundred fifty times twenty-three? I hadn't realized there *were* so many minutes in the day. This is the kind of calculus we do now, in our so-called information age. There are other numbers to consider:

we may check our phones 150 times a day, but we *touch* our phones about 2,617 times, according to a separate 2016 study, conducted by Dscout, a research firm. Apple has confirmed that users *unlock* their iPhones an average of eighty times per day. I don't know about you, but I now get unpleasant little messages informing me of the number of hours I've spent on my screen so far each day, and how that number compares with my daily screen time "goal." At some point, apparently, I had signed up for "Moment," an app that mercilessly tracks my every on-screen minute. It sends me text alerts when I least expect them, conveying such mixed messages as: "You're over your goal of 42 pick-ups today. But it's no big deal." These alerts do not motivate me to rein it in. They simply serve as a reminder, multiple times per day, of what I could have achieved in the last eleven years, if I'd never bought an iPhone.

Jaron Lanier, the computer scientist and author who is often called the "father of virtual reality" for his innovating work in that field, reflects on this very point in his memoir, *Dawn of the New Everything.* When he came up in the Silicon Valley of the 1980s, it was still early days, and nothing about the culture of technology felt inevitable. He addresses his lay readers, us, the general public: "You let us reinvent your world! I'm still curious why."

I gravitated to voices like Lanier's, people who pushed back against the monolith of big tech and its dehumanizing designs, even when they themselves operated from inside the industry (all the better, in fact, if they did). I had been vaguely embarrassed, for most of our young century, to admit just how much enmity I experienced toward almost everything to do with the Internet.

I was born in 1982, sliding into the tail end of the demographic that could describe life so far as neatly split between before and after. I grew up on paper. Then, at some point in the middle of high school: The arrival of a boxy beige Macintosh desktop that looked more than a little like E.T. The stress and fear associated with its moods and glitches and propensity for erasing my just-finished assignments. At the same time: its reassuringly rudimentary soul. The computer didn't seem like much of an invading army back then. After all, it could barely find the printer.

By the time I hit the end of adolescence, though, that creaky desktop had been replaced by a nifty, colorful Macintosh laptop, one with a cool blue rubber casing, signaling youth, heralding the future. I was on a rapidly escalating schedule now: from beeper to flip phone to BlackBerry to iPhone, staring into glowing screens of all sizes for more and more of every day. But with each echelon of progress achieved, I was acutely aware of the casualties, the old habits, the silent stretches, the hours when no one could reach me, or bother me, or tell me how I should be spending my time. All fallen by the wayside. In the early days of our digital life, I had been the doomsday old crone in a twenty-year-old's body, rolling my eyes at the new code of behavior I witnessed online. I was stunned by the immodesty of it. I still am. But I halfheartedly created a Facebook profile, back when I foolishly assumed it would soon go away, once we all got bored with it.

In the years that followed, with Silicon Valley's ascendancy so astonishingly unopposed, it became painful to talk about certain things. For example: books. I kept it to myself, how books had saved my life, again and again. Alone in Paris, age twenty-one, spiking Diet Coke with airplane bottles of vanilla vodka while reading a crumbling copy of *The Counterlife* I had bought on the banks of the Seine. Sublimely absorbed by Janet Malcolm's *The Silent Woman* on my sofa on Ninth Street, in the days after a painful breakup. These moments. So many moments, a lifetime of them. Reading was one of the great revelations of getting off the Adderall: how much more it turned out I could take in, ironically, *without* my focus pills. More subtext. More feeling. More meaning.

It felt dangerous to harp on about the sacred act of reading, as it was books—our very ability to read them—that seemed most threatened by the invasion of Silicon Valley technology. Books felt like the number-one target that those glassy creatures of efficiency had in their sights.

Witness "Blinkist," an app with a reported $35 million of venture capital invested in it at the time of this writing. The goal? Distill nonfiction books down to a list of "take-aways" that would require no more than fifteen minutes to absorb. I imagine the young techies in a room, coming up with this idea, proudly advocating the goal of chopping up nonfiction into forgettable summaries. I find I can picture the scene all too clearly. I consider what it would look like for some of my favorite books to be submitted to this dressing-down. How would Huxley's *Doors of Perception* fare? Perhaps something like this:

One day in Southern California, Aldous Huxley swallowed mescaline, found his grey trousers mesmerizing, the books on his shelf beautiful, and time irrelevant. He concluded: there's a Mind at Large.

Not quite poetry, but at least you don't have to waste your time reading the book. I imagined a future where books became decorative, inert, and then, eventually, when no one could make any money from publishing them, simply disappeared. Our consolation prize? iPads. Alexa. The expensive gadgets of the future, whatever they may be.

But actually, by the time I returned to San Francisco, the national mood regarding that pastel-colored city had begun to sour. A recent cover of *Wired* had displayed Mark Zuckerberg's face, bruised, bloodied, and bandaged, clammy with sweat, his light green eyes fixated on some middle-distance target, rigid with panic. Or, at least, a billionaire's version of panic. The cover artist responsible for this image explained that his blending "fact and fiction" was a perfectly apt continuation of Zuckerberg's own practices, the ones that had helped enable "fake news" to conquer the American electorate.

Since the 2016 election, Zuckerberg and Facebook had taken a dive in the public's estimation, most specifically for revelations that an independent contractor named Cambridge Analytica had deployed Facebook users' personal information to directly influence their political leanings. In 2018, Zuckerberg appeared before Congress to testify about Facebook's role in exposing its users to this kind of covert manipulation. Watching the proceedings was deeply illuminating: it turned out that many of our senior-most lawmakers simply did not understand the technological revolution that had already conquered our country, our citizenry, and our brains. Orrin Hatch, the Republican senator from Utah, epitomized this chasm when he asked, "If users don't pay for your service," how does Facebook make money? Zuckerberg replied, "Senator, we run ads."

Zuckerberg was in Washington to defend his company's invasion of our privacy, not its death grip on our attention, but in a sense, that latter accusation too was implicit in the new, anti-Facebook pushback. Now that our covenant with Facebook had been breached by the data privacy revelations, all aspects of the relationship were open to question.

I had come to San Francisco, in part, to visit a new friend, Franklin, who was getting his PhD in computer science at Stanford, a candidate in the same program that had hosted so many of the technologists that now shape our lives. Google legends Larry Page and Sergey Brin; the founder of LinkedIn, Reid Hoffman; Kevin Systrom and Mike Krieger, friends at Stanford who together created Instagram: the list goes on.

I'd met Franklin a few months before, on New Year's Eve, 2017. In the course of our conversation, I discovered that he was so immersed in his work that he kept his phone on airplane mode all day, every day. As a result, he had never heard of the Me Too movement and could hardly identify Harvey Weinstein. "He's a producer, right?"

I looked at him in disbelief, trying to determine whether he was kidding. All around us, for the last three months, our friends and acquaintances, to say nothing of the anonymous hordes on social media, had talked of little else.

"Everyone I know does the same thing," he told me. "You can't do this kind of elite work otherwise. When your phone is on and receiving communications, your IQ automatically drops ten points." (Indeed, a 2005 study commissioned by Hewlett-Packard publicists and carried out by King's College London found just that, describing "infomania" as more than twice as deleterious for IQ as cannabis.)

In Palo Alto, Franklin led me through the majestic Spanish architecture to the William Gates Computer Science Building. We passed human-sized robots on the first floor ("It's incredible how far we've come, yet they can't get that robot to use his hand to pick up a simple object," he observed) and ascended to the more unremarkable hallways of offices upstairs. We stopped next to a young woman, a friend of Franklin's. Hunched over her laptop, she wore enormous headphones over her apparently unbrushed hair. Next to her, an empty pizza box lay open on the table. Removing her headphones for a moment, she told us she was studying an algorithm that had recently come under fire in the press. Developed at Stanford, this algorithm was used by judges and bail bondsmen to predict criminal recidivism. Many outside of Silicon Valley considered it racist. She had gone back to look at its raw components again. I took the opportunity to ask her if she also practiced Franklin's extreme discipline with personal technology.

"Oh, not at all," she said. "I look at my phone the second I wake up every morning and I keep looking at it all day."

"You do?" Franklin asked her, clearly surprised. "So what's your strategy?"

"I don't have one. I just constantly feel bad," she said.

Her confession cheered me up. Even in the literal hallways of elite computer scientists, I was her and she was me, united in our constant badness. I shot her a sympathetic smile as she went back to her algorithms.

In fact, this very computer science department, which has helped to staff many of Silicon Valley's most influential companies, has also produced the occasional techie apostate. The most prominent example in recent years: Tristan Harris. I'd been following him with real interest, as Tristan Harris was one of the few people who, for great stretches of 2016, 2017, and 2018, actually gave me hope. I had assumed that the fight was already over and that Big Tech had won, but Harris seemed an antidote to the complacency with which we had greeted the introduction of Silicon Valley's prerogatives into our pockets and our brains.

Harris had come into the public eye in the last three years, operating as a whistleblower, flagging for the general public the addictive, attention-stealing properties of technology design. Dubbed by *The Atlantic* "the closest thing Silicon Valley has to a conscience," Harris, still in the first half of his thirties, had already become a fixture on a certain circuit, giving a TED Talk, featured on *60 Minutes,* appearing at chic conferences such as South by Southwest, making use of every high-profile opportunity to warn that the software on our devices is explicitly designed to be irresistible. What we are facing, he says, is nothing less than an "existential threat" from our own devices.

Harris should know: he first learned these persuasive design techniques at Stanford, studying in B. J. Fogg's infamous laboratory. Harris, in his talks and writings, lays out examples of these kinds of techniques, widely implemented to keep us glued to our phones and computers (to say nothing of our iPads and Apple Watches). These include almost every aspect of design we've grown accustomed to: from the fact that Facebook automatically labels its messages "read," obliging a quick response for fear of offending the sender; to YouTube's automatically playing the next video and the next video and the next; to Snapchat's "streak" statistic; to Twitter's algorithm operating to confirm your worldview, not challenge it. But Harris's larger argument is that it's not just these design details that nudge us toward tech addiction, but the framing itself. Our devices claim to represent the whole picture, offer us *all* the possible choices, thereby defining our very sense of the world.

Harris observed many of these persuasive technology practices directly when he sold his start-up company to Google and became a Google employee himself. There, he worked on the Gmail team, and wondered why none of his colleagues seemed interested in the question of how to create a product that did not take over our lives.

Harris has repeatedly argued that our phones work like the single most addictive Las Vegas technology: slot machines. Pulling a lever and receiving, at unpredictable moments, a reward—like an email bearing fabulous news, or a Twitter notification, or ten likes on your new Instagram photo—has been shown to captivate the human brain more than any other system or schedule.

The sociologist Natasha Dow Schüll explored exactly what makes slot machines so hypnotic, in her 2012 book, *Addiction by Design*. What she found was that it was not, contrary to expectation, the possibility of winning that keeps users mesmerized for hours on end, day after day, pulling levers and pushing buttons. Rather, it's the very feeling of being in a suspended reality outside of daily life, "that machine zone" where "nothing else matters," as one of Schüll's subjects put it. This zone is so powerfully seductive that Schüll, in the course of her reporting, heard of many gamblers who chose to wear diapers in order to avoid having to leave the slot machine for a bathroom break. To me, that slot-machine trance perfectly encapsulated the sensation of scrolling on my phone: the passive twilight state, not quite aware, not quite asleep, in which life itself, with all its uncertainties and obligations, can be put on hold.

Our phones and our slot machines both conjure that spell in part through a formula the behaviorist B. F. Skinner called "variable ratio reinforcement." Working first with rats, then later with pigeons, Skinner developed and honed the optimal schedule with which to instill new behaviors in animals. He found that when his pigeons were rewarded with food pellets on an unpredictable schedule—sometimes pellet, sometimes nothing—that very unpredictability kept them coming back to the lever far more often than if they received the food pellet every time—and for far longer. This is now the logic by which many of the apps on our phone hold us captive: Will we have a new like? A new note? A new notification? Some tiny little source of surprise and validation that makes us feel loved or needed? We never know what we're going to find when we pick up our phone and begin to scroll. That very not-knowing is one of the stickiest features of our personal technology.

Skinner argued that there was no good reason to keep wasting time on thoughts and feelings, as psychology had been doing for almost a century, when behavior could be controlled by simple tweaks to the external environment. More than sixty years later, the principles of variable ratio reinforcement are a topic of discussion in Silicon Valley, informing a wide swath of technology's design, down to Mark Zuckerberg's thought process whenever he tinkers with his secret algorithms. And of course, in this scenario, it is us, the Facebook users of the world, who are the pigeons. I don't know about you, but I resent that terribly.

"You could say that it's my responsibility" to practice self-control over digital devices, Tristan Harris told Bianca Bosker of *The Atlantic* in 2016, "but that's not acknowledging that there's a thousand people on the other side of the screen whose job is to break down whatever responsibility I can maintain."

In the curiously amoral, business-as-usual atmosphere in which persuasive technology proliferated, Harris wanted to wake us all up. It began in 2013, when, still working at Google, he assembled a presentation he called "A Call to Minimize Distraction & Respect Users' Attention" and uploaded it onto Google's internal server. To his surprise, it caught on immediately. Everyone was reading it. He had articulated what many at the company knew or feared was true. "Never before in history have the decisions of a handful of designers (mostly men, white, living in SF, age 25–35) working at 3 companies had so much impact on how millions of people around the world spend their attention," Harris wrote, punctuating his message with catchy images and photos. "We should feel an enormous responsibility to get this right."

After his PowerPoint presentation shot through Google, Harris was given a different job title: design ethicist, a role perhaps unique to Google, and in and of itself quite revealing. In his new role, he tried to push for a company-wide change in sensibility, going as far as inviting Thich Nhat Hanh—the same legendary Buddhist monk whose meditation retreat was briefly attended by David Foster Wallace—to Google's Mountain View campus. Now in his nineties, Nhat Hanh had written and spoken about his increasing worry that technology was hurting human relationships, causing isolation and loneliness, and distracting us from ourselves. In his speeches and writing, Nhat Hanh sometimes relays this parable:

"There is a Zen story about a person sitting on a horse, galloping very quickly. At a crossroads, a friend of his shouts, 'Where are you going?' The man says, 'I don't know, ask the horse!' This is our situation. The horse is technology. It carries us and we cannot control it. So we have to begin with intention, asking ourselves, what do we want?"

The famous and famously busy monk accepted Harris's invitation, provided that Harris round up some of Google's most influential employees for the meeting. Harris described the proceedings to the journalist Ezra Klein: on one side of the conference room table, Harris and colleagues, including the Google Glass and Gmail teams. On the other, Thich Nhat Hanh surrounded by eight bald monks in their colorful robes. Nhat Hanh had come with a list of requests he wanted to put to the Google engineers, ways for them to help humanity through design. "They really did see that the phone was tearing apart family relationships," Harris said. But Nhat Hanh's number-one request to the Google big shots: come attend his meditation retreat in Plum Village, France.

"His whole point is that most people in the tech industry

have never gone inward, into their own inner experience, in a deep way," Harris told Klein. "He saw that that was the prerequisite for making different decisions about how this technology environment should be designed." Nhat Hanh was offering the chance to go inward, to go deep.

"Unfortunately," Harris added, "I don't think anyone went."

Harris stayed in his job as design ethicist for two and a half years. He quit in 2016, convinced that it was not possible to enact meaningful reform from inside the company. He left to work as a human "alarm system," traversing the country to change the hearts and minds of both consumers and technologists themselves. Outside Google's fortressed walls, Harris quickly gained public attention with his lofty, aspirational slogan: "Time Well Spent." That's what he craved and what he sought— and what he felt we should too. No more mindless hours scrolling bottomless social media feeds in a self-loathing stupor; no more unconsciousness when checking email or responding to texts.

Harris himself had so internalized his own motto that he had become quite difficult to get in touch with. On his website, he had issued the following caveats and clarifications:

I get hundreds of requests and I'm drowning in communication— you can help me to prioritize your message by contacting me using Shortwhale.

Please note:

- Sorry, I am not available for getting coffee.
- Please do not ask me about smartphone productivity, tips & tricks.

When I went instead to Shortwhale, as Harris instructed, I discovered yet another pleading collection of reasons not to try to get in touch with him.

> Hi! Thanks for reaching out. Due to overwhelming incoming requests and our need to be laser-focused on changing the dangerous incentives of technology platforms—I am unable to manage my email.
>
> To be most effective, and for my health and sanity, I am cutting down on the time I spend responding to emails to the absolute minimum . . .
>
> If you want to invite me to give a talk, please be aware that I get *hundreds* of invitations per month and I have to be very selective about where I can have the most impact.

In the end, it took me months to meet Harris—and a trip to Colorado. We met in the courtyard of the swanky St. Regis hotel in Aspen, both there to attend the Aspen Ideas Festival, he as a speaker, I on a reporting assignment. It was an idyllic summer morning, the deep green mountains ringing my peripheral view. Harris arrived at 10:00 a.m. exactly. With a slight build and dark red hair, he was dressed in a standard-issue Silicon Valley power ensemble: Rag & Bone button-down, Allbirds sneakers. His clothes bespoke the efficiency of "Time Well Spent," a uniform chosen for its simplicity and versatility.

"Should we go inside?" I asked him, gesturing toward the construction noise that was penetrating our mountain-view reverie. "Why, because I'm so attentionally sensitive?" he asked, smiling. "Oh, well, no. Because I am," I said. We chose the view and stayed in place. I was acutely aware that we now had twenty-nine minutes left to us. Harris placed his well-worn black Moleskine notebook on the table and ordered an ice coffee.

"When you see a system that is plowing ahead with this engine of five hundred billion dollars of market value based on a business model that *is* eroding the fabric of our society—it feels like there's no way to—like, how are you going to adjust a system that's that powerful?" he began. "The deepest way to change a system is to change the mind-set or paradigm in which people are seeing the situation."

For instance, Harris points to the two dominant and contradictory stories we hear about Facebook: One, a fundamentally constructive, positive company that's "connecting the world." Two, an attention-stealing, algorithmic master manipulator "supercomputer," pointed at users' brains, "that's going to play chess against their mind." Despite the Facebook slogans promising a pro-social agenda, Harris had come to see that the company's daily mission was, in essence, "a game for our attention." In this, it was no different from Google, from Instagram, from Path, from Zynga, from countless other Silicon Valley behemoths.

"There's a whole part of the tech industry called growth hacking, and it's common, and it's basically: How do you engineer growth? And it's basically a psychology manipulation team. So everyone in the industry knows that this is how it works, it's just people in the public who don't know," Harris told me. "Making the world more open and connected, or standing up for truth, is *not* what Facebook's thousands of engineers go to work to do every day."

I asked Harris whether he was more concerned with galvanizing consumer awareness or industry reform. "Both. Both. Because we have limited time and this is an urgent problem, we have to speak in a way that reaches everybody, so the metaphors we aim for are things that anybody can understand. We make no assumptions about people understanding privacy and data rights. Forget it. How do we make it simple? There's a situation that we're in which is not really aligned with the human environment, which is to say parent-child relationships, relationships with ourselves, the face time that we need to have with each other and community. We don't have a technology environment that's designed to support those things. It's just move fast and break things, tear it all apart, suck attention out of each of those ecosystems. So when you see it that way as a consumer, you think, oh my god, it really is playing chess against my mind."

Harris had recently launched a new venture: the Center for Humane Technology. It had a website, but I could not discern the grand plan to save us from our phones. Every Sunday, I received its discreet once-a-week newsletter, which consisted of the latest message board comments. To read them, of course, required my investing even more screen time.

Harris says he struggles with the tension between the small fixes and the big picture. If he makes concrete suggestions for managing one's personal technology use—like keeping your phone in grayscale at night to make it less alluring, for example—that can endanger his mission to keep an urgent focus on the existential threat that he believes tech poses. "Even if I just mention offhand 'grayscale,' people start to pin us as 'Oh, the Center for Humane Technology is trying to give people tips about how to use their devices.' As opposed to: we're trying to avoid catastrophe."

I asked Harris when this consciousness had first developed in him, this desire to help save us from our screens. Somewhat sheepishly, he said Burning Man, referring to the annual desert bacchanal, but then said what a cliché that was as an answer and that he's already told interviewers that story, and besides, it isn't even true; he's always wanted to change the world. He has always cared.

Harris encounters a recurring counterpoint: The skeptics. The people who argue that what we are living through is no different, fundamentally, from any of the technological disruptions throughout history. I had actually seen such a conversation unfold the day before, when Harris was interviewed onstage by a journalist who was unconvinced, he said, that our technology had fundamentally changed anything. The skeptics will almost inevitably mention the Gutenberg printing press and the hand-wringing that ensued in its wake. People had been horrified: How will a printing press change the nature of scholarship? For skeptics such as these, there's no good evidence that our current moment is uniquely dangerous—or even unique.

"Training your attention on a complex problem, you could get stuck in a debate about what is truth? How do we know something is true? Who is to say what's true?" Harris said. "We have a limited amount of time to solve this tech problem, so if you allow the conversation to get steered that way, and you're not aware that your attention is being pulled into a debate area that actually misses the fact that there's a catastrophe . . . It's like being on the *Titanic* and you're getting into a debate about which direction you're going. It's like the boat is *sinking*. We don't want to get into a philosophy conversation about which way we're going."

At exactly thirty minutes past the hour, Harris said goodbye, rose from the table, and walked across the St. Regis's courtyard to his next appointment: with Chris Cox, then the chief product officer of Facebook. From my seat, I watched the two handsome thirtysomething men spend the next half hour convivially talking, smiling, and laughing. I changed to a closer table to get out of the sun. When Chris Cox rose to leave, I'm almost certain I heard him say "Thanks for keeping us in check with all this." Their deep collegiality was evidently unaffected by Harris's habit of traveling the country comparing Facebook to a "super-computer pointed at our brains," addicting us with its constant and careful manipulations. Watching their conversation from across the courtyard was as clear a demonstration as any that Harris in fact occupies a comfortable position in the technology industry's pecking order, that there is ample room for a whistle-blower like him; and perhaps even a healthy business opportunity for big tech companies in adopting—or pretending to, at least—Harris's mission of Time Well Spent.

For the fact is, increasingly, Harris is not alone. There is by now a chorus of like-minded voices chiming in, tech insiders who have seen behind the curtain and feel it is their appointed duty to warn the rest of us. The examples are numerous and well-known: Chamath Palihapitiya, Facebook's former head of user growth, bluntly stated in a speech at Stanford's business school that "we have created tools that are ripping apart the social fabric of how society works. That is truly where we are." (He later walked back this remark after it generated an uproar. And yet.) Sean Parker, Facebook's former president, admitted to being afraid of what social media is "doing to our children's brains." Addictiveness is built into Facebook's very design, he said, a "social-validation feedback loop" that plays into basic human vulnerabilities. Just as Steve Jobs and Bill Gates had both strictly limited their children's access to their devices, by 2017, it had become increasingly popular for the Technorati to send their own kids to tech-free schools, wanting for them not shiny iPad screens, but old-fashioned, tactile finger paints, wooden blocks, and paper books. It is only outside of Silicon Valley that we turn such a blind eye to the effects of unmitigated technology on developing brains.

One voice on par with Tristan Harris in terms of urgency is Harris's former Google colleague James Williams. I first saw

Williams mentioned in an article in *The Guardian,* about technology addiction. At that time, I was immersed in all things William James, and couldn't contain my delight at the coincidence of names. By the time I got in touch with Williams, a little less than a year later, it was shortly after the Cambridge Analytica Russian hacking data breach revelations. And Williams had moved to Moscow, of all places. His wife had been posted there by her job at the UN, he told me. In the current political climate, Williams was nervous about publicizing their current location. He peered into his computer monitor, his face pale from the glow. He was my same age, mid-thirties, with a round face behind thick glasses. He was chewing thick brown crackers as he addressed himself to his camera.

Williams and Harris overlapped at Google, but Williams worked there longer, having arrived at the company in the early 2000s, in what could still be called the early days. At that point, steeped in idealism, Google's founders talked about how they were going to reject the standard advertising model that had debased so much of American life. They would do it differently, they'd offer something better, more enlightened, rather than the "blasting stuff out at people . . . distraction thing" of yore, as Williams puts it. But, he says, this attitude changed, prompted by two different inflexion points in the company's history: when Google acquired YouTube and felt pressured to make an enormous profit; then, with the release of the iPhone, in 2007, when Google left the boundaries of our desks and entered our pockets. This is what Williams tells me: within a few years into his employ at Google, working on the search advertising team, "we lost that narrative of we're changing what advertising is." Google dove into the Silicon Valley game of ruthlessly competing to monetize its users' attention. In many ways, it has emerged as the clear victor.

"The liberation of human attention may be the defining moral and political struggle of our time," Williams writes in the beginning of his eloquent book about the digital age, *Stand Out of Our Light*. The short book is the product of his time at Oxford, where he went after he left Google, to study the ethics and philosophy of technology at the prestigious Oxford Internet Institute.

By the summer of 2018, Williams had earned his doctorate in philosophy and was awaiting clarity on his next career move. I was eager to talk to him about his book, which hewed as closely to my own experience of the digital age as any single thing I'd read. Describing his time at Google, Williams writes:

I felt . . . distracted. But it was more than just "distraction"—this was some new mode of deep distraction I didn't have words for. Something was shifting on a deeper level than mere annoyance, and its disruptive effects felt far more perilous than the usual surface-level static we expect from day-to-day life. It felt like something disintegrating, decohering: as though the floor was crumbling under my feet, and my body was just beginning to realize it was falling. I felt the story of my life being compromised in some fuzzy way I couldn't articulate . . . Does that even make sense? It didn't at the time.

It made perfect sense to me.

Williams grew up in Abilene, Texas, studied literature as an undergraduate, and never for a second imagined he'd wind up working in advertising. Many people who go to work in tech, of course, think the same thing. They are full of brilliance and idealism, convinced they are going to work on the vanguard of the new. It is only when they show up for their jobs in Silicon Valley that they realize what they're really doing is selling ads all day, but in a much more invasive manner than ever before possible. Williams tells me that when Tristan Harris's presentation circulated through the company in 2013, the two connected and began to meet in various conference rooms, sketching out their shared ideas on Google's whiteboards. They both had a sense of urgency about what they were seeing around them.

"In the same way that you pull out a phone to do something and you get distracted and thirty minutes later you find that you've done ten other things except the thing that you pulled out the phone to do . . . There's fragmentation and distraction at that level, but I felt like there's something on a longer-term level that's harder to keep in view—that longitudinal sense of what you're *about*," Williams tells me.

He knew that among his colleagues, he and Harris weren't the only ones feeling this way. Speaking at a technology conference in Amsterdam, Williams asked the designers in the room, some 250 of them, "How many of you guys *want* to live in the world that you're creating? In a world where technology is competing for our attention?"

Not a single hand up.

"Does it surprise you that people aren't more up in arms about the hijacking of attention?" I asked Williams.

He paused. "Yes and no," he finally said. "The reason I'm not so surprised is I don't think we even have the right words for the effects this stuff is actually having on our lives."

I think back to Britt Anderson, who wrote the scientific paper with the eye-catching title: "There Is No Such Thing as Attention."

"We need the right terms if we are to say something meaningful," Anderson had argued, speaking for the research community. Was not the same thing true for the rest of us?

And this is what's most striking to me: in our jumbled, conflicted conversations, we are no longer just talking about the aggravation, the short-term woe, of struggling to focus on our day-to-day tasks. We are now, as well, talking about something far deeper and more fundamental. Williams offers us the metaphor of "starlight" and "daylight" to capture this existential erosion, for which he believes we don't yet have the right terms. Technology has done more than obscure the "spotlight" of our immediate attention: it has confused us on an individual level about the values we care about in our lives—our personal "starlight"—and on a societal one, about what we as a culture consider our shared truths. Our daylight.

And here I'm reminded of something Harris had said to me in Aspen. "Without shared truth or shared facts, you get chaos—and people can take control." He left that comment hanging. He did not need to specify. He did not need to spell it all out, he did not need to say: This is water. This is now our water.

9

Of course, I'm in as deep as anyone, as splintered, dependent, and distracted. I am jittery and incomplete without my phone, while simultaneously despising it, dropping it on the sidewalk at least once a day. It's an old dynamic, actually, needing and hating the same sublime substance. This conflicting state of push and pull was exactly what Adderall had reduced me to, years before.

I discovered the extent of my addiction when I traveled to Scotland with Josh, one August in the midst of my attention research. Josh had written a show that was running at the Fringe Festival, in Edinburgh, and I tagged along, still the newish girlfriend. We decided to take one trip outside Edinburgh, to the Hebrides islands, the famously lush, remote outcroppings on Scotland's western coast. We hadn't quite realized the trek required to get there: a train to Glasgow, a three-hour bus ride through the countryside, a two-hour ferry ride from the bus, to land on the Isle of Islay, with no car, no cell phone service, and, in many places, no sidewalks, just as a Scottish rainstorm rolled in. From below our umbrella, I looked around the beautiful landscape, sparsely populated, sheep dotting the gentle hills. With help from the local bus driver, we navigated toward the inn where we were staying. I was surprised that I felt a low-level anxiety when our phones did not budge on one crucial point: No Service. Arriving at the inn, we were told the Wi-Fi may or may not work. It depended on the hour, really, or the weather, or something. The innkeeper looked at us blandly, and with, I felt, a speck of judgment. He knew our kind. By now, I was fighting off panic. Would we ever get off this island again? The antlers hanging from the quaint inn's walls looked distinctly sinister. Visions of a Scottish horror movie: two vanishing American tourists only their families would miss.

What's the word for the opposite of this condition? This addicted, anxious, and splintered headspace? Maybe it's "flow." I am not here referring to white-water rafting. Rather, to the powerful, elusive state familiar to artists and athletes and anyone else who finds themselves so absorbed in the task at hand, they lose their sense of time, their sense of self, and experience only instinct and intuition. In flow, concentration is effortless and limitless.

The concept of flow was first popularized in the 1990s, by the psychologist Mihaly Csikszentmihalyi. In his seminal books on the subject, Csikszentmihalyi (pronounced: chick-sent-me-high) argued for the strong link between frequency of flow states and overall life satisfaction—a link now substantiated by further outside studies. "Happiness is not something that happens. It is not the result of good fortune or random chance," he writes in *Flow*. "Attention is our most important tool in the task of improving the quality of experience."

Indeed, astonishingly, in the studies conducted on "flow," no single factor appears as clearly correlated to a sense that one's life has meaning as regularly experiencing flow. Actually, I understood why. After all, every minute in flow is a blessed departure from the minutia of routine, of ego, of anxiety, and of doubt. It's a chance to tap into that underground power we sense in ourselves, yet so frequently fail to find. Csikszentmihalyi's work on the importance of cultivating flow continues to resonate: his books are perennial bestsellers; his TED Talk, "Flow, the Secret to Happiness," has been viewed more than five million times.

For the attentional magic known as flow, I had a name of my own. I called it the Place of Deep Absorption. It was not to be taken for granted. It was not gained lightly. But a good writing day depended on getting there. And a really good day meant staying awhile, gaining confidence, turning this way and that, with room to be rash. On these rare days, with this attentional wind at my back, the pages I wrote would pour out of me and inevitably wind up, largely unedited, in the final book or article. The problem was the rarity. The Place of Deep Absorption was in fact a different realm entirely from the dreary environs where I usually dwelled, fretting over unanswered email at a messy desk in Brooklyn, about to get a stomachache. It was rare and, I feared, thumbing through Instagram, getting rarer still.

In the almost thirty years since the publication of *Flow,* others have periodically come on the scene attempting to augment or reinvent the idea. Jamie Wheal is one of them. I had first heard about Wheal at the psychedelic conference in Oakland, because he'd come there to give a speech. He seemed to appeal, in particular, to a psychedelic set, a Silicon Valley set, and the very real intersection of those two populations.

Wheal, a self-help leader, founded the Flow Genome Project in order to teach humans how to "hack flow" and to achieve "peak performance." He had created a following all based on the flow-related pursuits he offered: expensive flow camps in the summer, flow courses online, and mass emails suggesting such techniques as:

- Maximizing VO2 with nasal flushes and turbines
- The interrelationship between nitrogen, nitric, and nitrous oxides (and which does what where)
- Easy hacks to trigger the mammalian dive reflex

Wheal had also written a book on the subject of flow, coauthored with the journalist Steven Kotler. By now, at least four different people had asked me if I'd read it, and all in the same tone: *You have to read this.* It was called *Stealing Fire.* I was getting the sense that these people considered it to be some kind of revolution in consciousness. With no small degree of skepticism, I procured a copy and prepared to find out for myself what a term like "revolution in consciousness" could possibly mean.

Wheal and Kotler argue that the time has come for us to take our brains and minds into our own hands, to learn to catapult ourselves into "non-ordinary states," like flow states, group flow, psychedelic states, all of which are the only kinds of states in which we can really hope to deal with the "wicked, complex problems" that confront us in our modern digital age. "Flow cuts the path to mastery in half and accelerates performance by up to 500%," Wheal had promised, on his weekly Webinar. Wheal and Kotler point out that the need to get out of our humdrum brains and into an exalted plane of non-ordinary attention is already well understood by a wide range of organizations and individuals, including the Navy SEALs.

Stealing Fire is, at bottom, a manifesto, an urgent communiqué for self-empowerment whose breathless, italicized claims sometimes intrigued me, sometimes annoyed me. Still,

I couldn't deny the power of some of Wheal and Kotler's message. Take, for instance, the question of the "umwelt."

"*Umwelt,*" they write, "is the technical term for the sliver of the data stream that we normally apprehend. It's the reality our senses can perceive. And all umwelts are not the same. Dogs hear whistles we cannot, sharks detect electromagnetic pulses, bees see ultraviolet light—while we remain oblivious." It is what William James was getting at when he wrote that "our normal waking consciousness, rational consciousness as we call it, is but one special type of consciousness, whilst all about it, parted from it by the filmiest of screens, there lie potential forms of consciousness entirely different." It refers to the inescapable limitation of our conscious processing. Or, perhaps, not so inescapable. Wheal and Kotler argue that in non-ordinary states, we can "perceive and process more of what's going on around us and with greater accuracy. In these states, we get upstream of our umwelt. We get access to increased data, heightened perception, and amplified connection." Our umwelts, in other words, can expand dramatically, absorbing with incredible, effortless attention a new universe of details. And, god knew, my umwelt needed help. It was, I often felt, an umwelt in shambles, a withered excuse for an umwelt, passively reacting to the spew of Internet-age ephemera thrown its way, increasingly shutting out the essential grandeur I knew was still there, in the corners of things, struggling to come up through the cracks.

The original flow philosopher, Csikszentmihalyi, writes in a much different tenor than Wheal and Kotler. Csikszentmihalyi describes the potential for directed attention to infuse meaning and joy into any human life. I have to admit that when I first began reading him, I didn't realize he was still alive. Quickly, I called to make an appointment. And on a chilly, overcast afternoon, I arrived in Claremont, California, at the small, wood-paneled house known as the Quality of Life Research Department, of Claremont Graduate University. It was about a twelve-minute drive from where David Foster Wallace had lived and died.

Csikszentmihalyi, now in his eighties, was standing in the foyer, at first perhaps not entirely certain as to who I was. Tentatively, he approached, and ushered me into his office, every desk, every cabinet, every inch of which was covered with precarious towers of loose papers, books, and manuscripts. He took his seat across from me, and we looked at each other over the collection of papers between us. White-haired and white-bearded, with twinkly, do-no-harm blue eyes and a stocky build, he had at this point in life accrued a kind of Santa Claus quality, if Santa were a fiercely brilliant Hungarian intellectual. He knew only vaguely of Wheal and his Flow Genome Project, he told me. He was accustomed, by now, to the periodic efforts he'd observed through the years of figures stepping forward to use or reinvent his foundational ideas on flow. "Luckily, most of the time these appropriations don't work out and they disappear," he told me.

"When did the seed of flow first plant itself in your mind?" I asked, shifting topics.

"Looking back, it was the experience of World War II," he said.

His father, he explained, was a Hungarian diplomat, and for the first half of the war, the family lived in Fiume, a city then in northern Italy that is now part of Croatia. Because Fiume had a torpedo factory, the Allies bombed it constantly, and the family slept in the basement every night. Finally, with his mother and sister, Csikszentmihalyi returned to Budapest to sit out the second half of the war—until the Soviets started bombing Hungary. But in the midst of these experiences, he tells me, his uncle taught him how to play chess.

"I discovered that when I played chess, the fact that looking out the window you saw dead people in the street and streetcars with pieces of a house sticking out of it, the beams spearing through the streetcar, and houses on fire . . ." He paused. "When I didn't play chess, that was real, but when I started playing chess, your attention is so focused on the game, you forget that this is happening outside." After the war, the family lived in a refugee camp. Throughout it all, Csikszentmihalyi recalls chess as the single sustaining experience. "The power of a game to fully engage your consciousness—that was interesting," he tells me, with his old-world understatement. I think, but don't remark, how surprising in some ways it is to hear this origin story. Flow, after all, can sound like a relic of the new age, or a highly privileged person's practice, another diversion for the bourgeois West to seek out with its disposable hours and income. Yet, in fact, "flow" as we know it today arose in dire circumstances, amid falling bombs and the assorted traumas of war. In a real way, flow saved the life of one eight-year-old boy.

It would take that boy more than forty years to write the first of his many books on the subject, even to understand that his childhood hours of rapt attention could be the basis of a new kind of philosophy, a new approach to finding meaning. "Attention is like energy in that without it no work can be done, and in doing work it is dissipated. We create ourselves by how we invest this energy," he would eventually write. "Control of consciousness determines the quality of life."

I knew I had to ask him about flow in the age of perpetual interruption. How did his ideas about deep, divine absorption change in the face of the buzzing, beeping technologies that have displaced all the old empty minutes? "In each new epoch—perhaps every generation, or even every few years, if the conditions in which we live change that rapidly—it becomes necessary to rethink and reformulate what it takes to establish autonomy in consciousness," he had written in *Flow,* published before he or anyone could have known the full extent of the information age coming our way. Yet the observation, from 1990, had struck me as prescient and stayed in my mind.

Before we broached the subject, I went out for a sip of water in the hallway lounge. In the minute or two I was gone, Csikszentmihalyi had taken out his slick silver laptop and now seemed hard-pressed to fully look away from its screen, even as he continued to narrate.

"It's much harder now to achieve that ability to focus," he told me, the laptop opened between us. "The distractions are rampant." His words sounded tired and canned, like he was mouthing an idea he didn't particularly care about. I pressed him again, but the subject clearly did not ignite him like memories of the distant past had done.

I became aware that hours had passed and I must take my leave if I hoped to make it back to Los Angeles in time for dinner. There was still so much more to discuss, but the drive back and various related obligations loomed in my mind. I stood to go. With a grim sense of irony, I registered that I was now rushing away from the actual *source* of "flow" to rejoin the soul-crushing rat race, otherwise known as the Southern California evening commute. It seemed all too appropriate, somehow, that there wasn't even time to finish the story.

Part III

INHERITANCE

10

When I boarded the plane from Los Angeles to Vancouver, I smiled to realize that I was going directly from one formidable Hungarian émigré to another: I was en route, at last, to see Gabor Maté in his home city. Months had passed since I sat cross-legged on the floor in Oakland, watching him address the psychedelic crowd. And though attention had been on my mind more or less constantly, I didn't feel any closer to insight or illumination. I still reached for my phone at every lull in the day, and in the lull between lulls.

By now, though, I had pored over the book Maté wrote on attention deficit disorder, *Scattered,* published in 1999, just as rates of ADHD diagnoses were skyrocketing in North America, with Adderall prescriptions tracing a path just behind. Right away, I saw that he was offering an unusual point of view, one that few in his field seemed to echo.

The prevailing model now for understanding attention deficit disorder is that of disease. In other words, ADHD is widely believed to be the result of a faulty brain, one you were born with. This framework is partially provided by the legacy of one book, published in 1994: *Driven to Distraction,* by the psychiatrists Ed Hallowell and John Ratey, a book that has sold more than two million copies to date. It did for attention deficit what Peter Kramer did for depression in *Listening to Prozac:* defined, crystallized, and medicalized an American moment, turning it immutably real. The authors' goal, stated in the opening pages of *Driven to Distraction,* is to remove all moral stigma from the diagnosis of attention deficit, to depict the condition as biological and probably genetic, to boot. There should be no more shaming of the underachievers afflicted with attention problems, no more urging them to just try harder: the authors point to research showing that activity in the prefrontal cortex—site of executive control—is sometimes damped down in subjects with the diagnosis as compared to those without; and, as well, that the size of the prefrontal cortex might be somewhat smaller in ADHD. Both findings could help to explain the disorder's signature impulsivity and attentional weak spots. Yet the research has not brought us to a point where one can be diagnosed with ADHD based on a brain scan or any other physical exam. Or even a single psychological assessment, which can often miss the diagnosis, they write.

I had long felt there was a curiously missing layer in conversations about ADHD. We invoke this acronym as if it were an explanation unto itself, the original, root cause of the problem, rather than a condition so steeped in the existential that a novelist would be hard-pressed to invent a more aptly modern disorder. And, in fact, one did: some version of ADHD could have been taken directly from the pages of Huxley's *Brave New World.* Yet I'd noticed that conversations on the topic of attention deficit seem oblivious to the almost metaphysical heart of the diagnosis.

Maté was the first person I'd encountered who talked about attention disorders in a different framework. "ADD is not a disease you inherit," Maté had told me. Rather, he explained, the trademark behaviors of ADD, like tuning out of the present moment, begin as coping mechanisms in early childhood. They begin as *useful* adaptations to one's environment. Later, through years of use, they calcify. They turn into problems, they become symptoms. But the diagnosis they often inspire, ADHD, doesn't consider their earliest emotional roots, only their persistent existence.

On the plane, I took out my highlighted, dog-eared copy of *Scattered* to gather my thoughts for the weekend ahead. The reason Maté became interested in attention at all, he writes, was that, at the age of fifty-three, he diagnosed himself with attention deficit disorder. This development had come as a revelation to him. At the time, outside his hours as a family doctor, he wrote a medical column for the Canadian newspaper *The Globe and Mail*. It was the early 1990s, when ADD was still a relatively unfamiliar condition in North America, even to most doctors. Yet when Maté began his research, he instantly recognized himself. "To dip my toe in was to know that, unawares, I had been immersed in it all my life, up to my neck. This realization may be called the stage of ADD epiphany, the annunciation, characterized by elation, insight, enthusiasm and hope. It seemed to me that I had found the passage to those dark recesses of my mind from which chaos issues without warning, hurling thoughts, plans, emotions and intentions in all directions."

He began self-medicating with Ritalin until he was officially diagnosed, and eventually switched from Ritalin to Dexedrine.

At the time, Adderall was not yet on the market. The Dexedrine, Maté writes, "made me more alert and helped me become a more efficient workaholic." Maté's early days on stimulants reminded me of my own: a spellbinding discovery about how life can be, an ecstatic breakthrough into a whole new land of possibility. "I felt euphoric and present, experienced myself as full of insight and love," he writes. Yet when his wife saw him on pills, the first thing she told him was: "You look stoned."

"Nobody is born with 'attention,'" Maté writes. "Like language or locomotion, being attentive is a skill we acquire. As with all other skills, the conditions necessary for the development of attention have to be present . . . There can be no expectation of owing or paying attention."

"The thing about attention," Maté had told me, "is that it requires the person to be in the present moment. People who have found the present moment very painful—one way to cope with that is to scatter your attention." I was startled by how unusual this point of view on attention seemed to be: the ability to pay attention is more typically portrayed in brain terms, or intellectual ones, not rooted in feelings at all.

"My three children also have attention deficit disorder," Maté writes. "In light of such a strong family history, it may seem surprising that I do not believe ADD is the almost purely genetic condition many people assume it to be. I do not see it as a fixed, inherited brain disorder but as a physiological consequence of life in a particular environment, in a particular culture. In many ways, one can grow out of it, at any age. The first step is to discard the illness model, along with any notion that medications can offer more than a partial, stopgap response."

Maté's argument that ADHD is not exclusively or even primarily genetic, not a simple matter of strands of DNA making their transit from one generation to the next, shouldn't be so unusual. After all, rates of ADHD have shot skyward in merely twenty years; genes do not change at such drastic rates, even over the course of decades. Yet the medical model by which most operate says that ADHD is a brain disease, largely genetic, treatable, not curable, with stimulant drugs like Adderall, Ritalin, and Vyvanse. It is medically controversial to question the disease model for ADHD, as doing so implies that for those afflicted, a different destiny is possible. But that doesn't stop Maté. "A kid with ADHD has no problem paying attention to video games," Maté told me. "The problem is not of attention, it's of motivation, of emotional motivation: whether we can be in the present moment or not. The more uncomfortable with ourselves, the more difficult it is to be in our skins, the more bored we get."

In his book, Maté argues that there's even a sense in which ADHD has become glorified, depicted as a source of innovation and discovery, associated with restless geniuses and other great disrupters. For example, he quotes Hallowell and Ratey, who write:

> The people who founded our country, and continued to populate it over time, were just the types of people who might have had ADD. They did not like to sit still. They had to be willing to take an enormous risk in boarding a ship and crossing the ocean, leaving their homes behind; they were action-oriented, independent, wanting to get away from the old ways . . . The higher prevalence of ADD in our current society may be due to its higher prevalence among those who settled America.

In this version of events, then, ADHD is the American pathology par excellence, and we should revere our ancestors' atypical brains as the force that inspired them to immigrate to the new world, having become entirely understimulated by the old one. "It's nonsense. How well do you survive as a hunter and a pioneer if you can't pay attention and stand still? It's just nonsense," Maté had remarked over Skype.

On that video call, I could see behind Maté to the contents of the bedroom in which he sat: a twin bed against the wall was covered in an Indian-print blanket; a kind of Peruvian shamanic tapestry hung on the wall. Maté's expression, in center screen, was dour. When we spoke, he had deflected my request to come see him. "Now is not a good time to ask me," he'd said. "I really need to pull back." Yet here I was on an airplane, a few months later, jammed in next to the strapping members of the Azusa Pacific University football team, who wore matching warm-up jackets and continually shouted "Schwartz!" throughout the flight, jarring me out of my semiconsciousness. The Schwartz in question, whose sizable head I could see in the row in front of mine, seemed to relish the attention.

A few hours after landing, I took my seat at the opening night of Maté's two-part workshop. With his son Daniel, he was hosting a weekend-long rethink of adult children–parent relationships. The Matés have called it "Hello Again: A Fresh Start for Parents and Their Adult Children."

From my seat, I watched Gabor train his gaze on his laptop screen, seemingly miles away, isolated in his concentration, preparing for the evening ahead. His body was small and lithe, without an extra pound to be seen; his shoes were sensible, orthopedic, prepared to carry him for miles, which one suspected they often did. There was a gravity to him that far exceeded his physical size. He was joined onstage by Daniel, whose own appearance, his curly hair untrimmed, his choice of tennis shoes and jeans, suggested a more disheveled, more playful quality, a fortysomething with his boyishness still intact.

"Were any of you here last year?" Gabor asked, by way of opening. "You might recall—we talked about this—that Daniel and I had a huge fight, driving down here. I just want to tell you that we worked it out. We're far more sophisticated this year, far more mature. We drove different cars to get here."

This would prove to be the tone the Matés took throughout the weekend's proceedings, displaying their father-son foibles for all to see, to relate to, to find solace in.

"I'm reading four books, two biographies each of Napoleon Bonaparte and Karl Marx," Maté continued. "I'm reading two biographies because in the case of Napoleon, one of the biographers just hates Napoleon, and the other guy makes a hero out of him. So I thought to get a full picture, I really need both perspectives.

"Now, Karl Marx's father—Karl was seventeen years old when he headed off to college. And his father writes to him the following: 'I want to see what I could have become had I come into the world under the same favorable auspices as you.' In other words: be the person I need you to be so that I can feel validated in my unfulfilled self. That's basically the message. Needless to say, Karl Marx then goes off and becomes a rebel and a radical journalist, and never makes a decent living. He was an incredible genius, but he never made a decent living in his life. He faced penury for the rest of his days." Gabor was building to one of his big themes: the parent who imposes his psychological needs on his child.

When Daniel's turn came, he traded places with his father at the lectern. It was Gabor who was well-known in Canada, who traveled the country speaking to sold-out audiences multiple times a week, not Daniel. I was curious to find out how the son would claim his own share of oxygen.

"I want to share a story, a personal anecdote from a few years ago, the way I remember it—and I stress the way I remember it—our memories are terrible for remembering what happened," Daniel began. "We were out to dinner at a gourmet, vegan-type place on Main Street that my parents had wanted to try. And I remember being kind of underwhelmed by the meal and I was maybe in a grumpy mood due to other factors . . . I don't remember the topic, but it was towards the end of the meal, and my father was saying *something* about *something*. That's all you need to know."

The audience laughed appreciatively and with some surprise at this irreverent treatment of Dr. Maté.

"I'm assuming it had something to do with personal development or meditation or spiritual health or physical health. Possibly I sensed that he wanted it to pertain to my life in some way and I made some kind of cutting remark. I don't remember the content, I wish I did, I'm sure it was very clever."

Throughout all this Gabor sat quietly in his chair, waiting for the story to unfurl. It was clear from the expression on his face that the two men had not rehearsed the evening's contents.

"The mood at the table abruptly shifted, and I couldn't tell where I had crossed the line exactly, but I had somehow crossed the line. And my dad, after composing himself, said to me: *You know, Daniel, there's a lot of wisdom in the Ten Commandments.*" Daniel paused for effect and the audience obliged him with laughter. *In particular, Daniel, the commandment admonishing us to honor our father and mother* . . .

"My mouth got very dry and my heart was racing and I said to him, *Dad, it sounds like I hurt your feelings, I didn't mean to hurt your feelings.* And he said, *No, Daniel, this isn't about my hurt feelings, I'm talking about you and your life."*

And so my weekend with the Matés began.

We reconvened the next morning in a large room at Simon Fraser University in downtown Vancouver. There were perhaps a hundred people there, seated at round tables set with white tablecloths. Taking out my notebook, I was startled to see that a woman at the next table over was crying, tears rolling down her cheeks in an endless cascade, her mouth twisted downward in an infinite frown. It was not quite 9:30 in the morning; the Matés, gathering themselves on the small stage, had yet to begin saying whatever it was they were planning to say. But I would soon understand that this kind of naked grief is the absolute norm when Gabor Maté enters a room.

"Sort of a disclaimer: I'm not a therapist. I'm not trained as a counselor," Daniel said, from the front of the room. "So that's clear, I don't present myself to be a therapist—but *he is,*" he said, gesturing toward his father.

"No, I'm not," said Gabor. "I've not had two minutes of training as a therapist ever. I've not studied at any institution that teaches therapy. I just do what I do."

In fact, this isn't quite how Maté sees it, as he has read extensively and learned directly from psychiatrists he admires, people such as Dan Siegel, Peter Levine, and Allan Schore, all of whom have worked on the question of brain development and trauma. Maté designed his own idiosyncratic training. In any event, the Matés' disclaimers didn't do anything to discourage the gathered attendees. For the next nine hours, all around me, these seemingly mild-mannered Canadians eagerly, urgently raised their hands for the roving microphones and described stories of everyday tragedy: alcoholic parents, addicted or deceased children, outright abuse, or something more subtle—the persistent feeling of not being *seen* by one's family, not being granted the permission for anything like authenticity.

As each person told their story, Gabor would leave the stage with his own roving mic and come to hover over them, sussing out by Socratic method the details of their experience. "What was the feeling associated with it?" he invariably asked. And however simple the question, it left many stumbling.

"I felt abandoned," someone might say.

"Excuse me, sorry, I need to interrupt you. That's not a feeling," Gabor repeated throughout the day, trying to bring them back to basics, to primal experiences of pure emotion, sadness or anger or rage, rather than more detached interpretations of those emotions, such as "I've been discarded" or "I'm not good enough." Later, I would ask him to explain why it was so important to get to the root feeling itself, separating it from the interpretation we form, the story our mind concocts to explain our feelings to ourselves. He told me that it's one's beliefs about what has happened, or the way someone else has behaved, that result in the feeling that afflicts them now—and, moreover, that those beliefs are often more informed by what's happened to us in the past than by what is happening in the present. If he can get the people who come to him in pain, in rage, to look at their beliefs, the feelings those beliefs have produced might shift. Indeed, it seemed the goal of each encounter that I observed over the course of that day was for the person, under the guidance of Maté's persistent, laser-like questioning, to come to see their history differently, whether in big ways or small.

"Trauma is not what happens *to* you," he repeated again and again. "It's what happens *inside of* you." It's the story you tell yourself about the experience you've had.

———

Maté is sometimes criticized for his relentless focus on "trauma," his sense that trauma is everywhere, underlying nearly all of the societal ills we see playing out in the press every day: the opioid crisis, the surprisingly large number of anxious, depressed, and suicidal teenagers. One of his most visible adversaries online is Stanton Peele, a psychologist specializing in addiction, who has taken after Maté in several different pieces. Writing in *Psychology Today,* in a piece called "The Trauma Searchers, Gabor Maté and Ted Cruz" Peele writes: "Maté—in his best selling book, *In the Realm of Hungry Ghosts*—insists that trauma is the root of all addiction . . . He demands that people examine their lives to uncover their trauma in order to explain their addictions. After that? Not much. Maté is essentially a psychoanalyst who claims that ferreting out childhood trauma solves psychological problems. No research supports this idea."

Peele argues that Maté's approach to addiction is reductionist, that seeing addiction so singularly through the lens of early childhood trauma and the changes to brain development that result is to miss the wider story of addiction. Yet Maté argues that far from overestimating trauma, the true state of things is that most people aren't ready to acknowledge just how much trauma exists all around us, bubbling toxically beneath the surface.

He often describes his own childhood: born in Budapest in 1944, to a twenty-four-year-old mother, whose husband was gone, disappeared into forced labor, whose parents and sister would soon be deported to Auschwitz. She came to feel that she had no choice but to pass her eleven-month-old son out of the Jewish ghetto, to a friend in hiding, where he lived apart from her until the Russians liberated Hungary.

Yet, for Maté, trauma isn't limited to overt acts of violence, neglect, or abuse, though these horrors are, he argues, more widespread than most people would guess. Trauma is just as much what happens to a child when their parents are too stressed out or depressed or distracted to be able to attune themselves to that child's emotional life, to be able to intuit what their child is feeling and respond to it. It is the good thing that didn't happen to you, as much as the bad thing that did. This too is trauma, he says, and it is an ever more common picture of life in the West, as parents, families, and neighborhoods are all increasingly splintered, communities eroded, individuals isolated.

The next day, a Sunday, I was dazed and lethargic. I hadn't realized how much it had taken out of me to sit in a room for nine hours listening to an anthology of tragedy and heartbreak, of devastated hopes and stuck lives. I lay in the bed in my hotel room well past noon with Maté's most recent and best-known book, *In the Realm of Hungry Ghosts,* which I had brought with me from New York, despite its significant bulk. It was Maté's magnum opus on addiction, a number-one bestseller in Canada when it was published. In it, he describes years of working with the drug addicts who spend their days on the streets in the Downtown Eastside neighborhood of Vancouver. That neighborhood, I realized, was not far from where I was staying. I pulled on my blue jeans and walked toward the setting that Maté describes.

I wound my way through Gastown, the expensive waterfront tourist district, where cashmere sweaters sell for five hundred dollars and cheerful, ruddy-cheeked crowds sip designer beer at outdoor cafés. Within two blocks of this consumer-culture paradise, the atmosphere changed dramatically, almost without warning. Now I was passing people in dirty, ragged clothing, lying together in clusters on the sidewalk. An image flashed into my mind: a pile of corpses. Within a minute, I saw the first syringe, flashing in the sunlight, a woman about to sink the needle into her flesh; or maybe she'd already removed it? There was a spurt of blood, exactly on cue, as if in a movie. But I was moving too quickly to parse the details. I was nervous, though perhaps I shouldn't have been, as most of the people I passed were too immersed in their own private dream worlds to seem fully aware of one another, much less me, a speed-walking gawker, tracing a path along the edge of the curb.

I hadn't understood that Vancouver's relatively mild climate, combined with its port, which historically provided an influx of drugs, has resulted in a neighborhood devoted to drug use: the Downtown Eastside. I found the address for the Portland Hotel, a drab, run-down-looking building, with downtrodden people clustered on the concrete just out front, others visible inside, through the dirty windows. I took in the bleakness of Maté's old surroundings. What had he felt when he came to work every day, when he looked at his patients tranced out and mumbling on the sidewalks all around him?

Apparently, he identified. "Hello, my name is Gabor, and I am a compulsive classical music shopper," he writes. In his book, he describes in detail an overwhelming need to acquire more and more CDs, an obsession that has dogged him for decades. "Some may find it difficult to understand how the desire to own six versions of Don Giovanni can be called an addiction," he acknowledges. I had to hand it to the man: the sheer chutzpah of comparing a compulsion to buy too many classical music recordings to the addictions of the people lying half dead on the street. Even I, who spent ten years addicted to prescription amphetamines, could not identify with what I was seeing. Maté knows it might sound absurd, but he earnestly defends the claim: "Once I spent eight thousand dollars in one week. I lied to my wife. I left a woman in labor at the hospital while I went to buy more CDs," I would hear him say. "I do not equate my music obsession with the life-threatening habits of my Portland patients. Far from it. My addiction, though I call it, wears dainty white gloves compared to theirs," he writes. "But if the differences between my behaviors and the self-annihilating life patterns of my clients are obvious, the similarities are illuminating—and humbling."

That night, I ate dinner over the turning pages of *Hungry Ghosts*. In its powerful, novelistic detail, it is unlike Maté's previous books. He filled the pages with vivid portraits of the people he encountered in his years on the Downtown Eastside, living on the street, addicted to drugs, who shout to him affectionately every day when he passes by: "Hey, Maté! Hey, Doc!" I could picture them so clearly, their voices ringing out from where they were sprawled on the sidewalk, or standing unsteadily, shuffling out strange dance moves on the pavement, as if to a song that no one else could hear. From Maté's pages, I absorbed their tragedies: the limbs they lost because they were too high to seek health care, the babies they forfeited, the jail time, the early deaths. This was the world Maté inhabited by choice for so long, this man who now gives TED Talks and gets paid significant sums to speak to audiences around the world.

Early the next morning, a taxi dropped me at Maté's home in a peaceful, leafy neighborhood of attractive two-story houses. I had extended my trip to come with him to one more day's events. It was a typical Monday, apparently, jammed with three different speeches he was scheduled to deliver. He answered the door in a burst of purposefulness. On the other hand, I was already on the verge of exhaustion, imagining the day's agenda, my backpack filled with protein bars and almonds in case of energy emergency. He let me in off his front porch. It seemed I had interrupted him while shaving. I waited for him downstairs. His home was cozy and warm, strewn with books and comfortable chairs to read them in.

We were picked up punctually by a woman with a British accent, with thick glasses and a nervous, obliging air. She was driving us out to a suburb called Abbotsford, where there was a small community college and a prison. Maté's talk that day was titled "Prisoners of Childhood: Reconciling Justice with Trauma History, Healing and Resilience." In the audience would be a mix of students and teachers as well as the formerly incarcerated, still rooted in the community.

In the front seat, he pulled out his laptop and trained his focus on his screen. I had the impression he was trying to disappear: our driver, the organizer of today's event, was an advocate in the Canadian women's prison system, and she had been talking ceaselessly in her high-pitched English accent since we got in the car about the injustices of the penal system, the bureaucratic realities she fights every day. As she continued on without pause, I noticed that Maté seemed miles away, hiding in his screen life.

Abruptly, he piped up, turning to our driver to ask: "So what do you want me to speak about today?" There was a loaded silence in the car as she processed that the event she had been planning for how many months, he seemed not to have prepared for at all. But she was too English and polite to let the extent of her anxiety show. They settled on some version of "the usual." Which I could by now infer meant trauma, all the ways in which we don't see or acknowledge it, all the ways in which it shapes us.

At once, Maté was animated again, present in the car with us. "You know there was this great quote in *The New York Times* this weekend by John le Carré about the trauma of being English. Wait a second, I have it right here . . ." Maté began flicking through the file of quotes he keeps at the ready on his iPhone. From an interview with John le Carré, he read:

"For our class in my era, public school was a deliberately brutalizing process that separated you from your parents, and your parents were parties to that. They integrated you with imperial ambitions and then let you loose into the world with a sense of elitism—but with your heart frozen." Yet the most striking comment came from le Carré's interviewer, Ben Macintyre, who threw in: "There is no deceiver more effective than a public-school-educated Brit. He could be standing next to you in the bus queue, having a Force 12 nervous breakdown, and you'd never be any the wiser."

In the back seat, I felt the chill of deep recognition. "I once dated someone who could have been the subject of that description," I said. Maté whipped around to look at me from his shotgun seat, his eyes bright and piercing. It was the first personal thing I had told him in our time together, and it seemed to have jolted him fully back into the present moment, doing what he loved: digging into the hot mess of being alive. "You know that whatever dysfunction was in him, that was perfectly matched by a dysfunction in you."

I could only laugh at the blatant truth of his observation.

In Abbotsford, Maté was led into a small conference room before his main speech. I trailed gingerly behind. Eight people sat around the table waiting for him. They were all former prisoners. Their crimes, they told us, by way of introduction, included prostitution, assault, drug dealing, and kidnapping. They would be telling their stories to a larger audience alongside Mate's own presentation. But first, they wanted a few minutes with Maté alone.

"I was seventeen when I started using," the woman to my right said. She was pretty, muscular, perhaps in her late forties. "That opened a whole world of violence, assault, prostitution."

"As a child, were you sexually abused?" Maté asked.

"Yes, I was."

He had told me previously that in all his years working with Vancouver's hard-core drug addict population, he had yet to meet a woman who hadn't been abused in childhood.

The woman next to me added that she had given birth to a little girl whom she had left behind, a little girl, she said, born addicted to heroin.

"Addiction is something different than dependence. Addiction involves dependence, but dependence is not always addiction," Maté said. "The difference is that with dependence, you might have physical withdrawal from a substance, but addiction involves actually a craving and repeating behavior and finding pleasure."

I thought I was beginning to understand one element of Maté's magnetic appeal: his lack of judgment.

"You just taught me something," the woman said. Her face had visibly brightened. There was some comfort to be found, it was clear, in the distinction between addiction and dependence, just a couple of degrees of freedom that she could be grateful for, a tiny bit less guilt.

When Maté took the stage a few minutes later, the eight former prisoners next to him, their very presence illustrated his main theme:

the omnipresence of trauma, throwing in neuroscience-heavy details about the impact of trauma on the brain, and how trauma impacts every aspect of life, including, notably, our very ability to pay attention.

This is a point Maté often emphasizes: his belief that ADHD is not a disease. Rather, he says, it *begins* as a perfectly normal, adaptive response to an abnormal situation. A few weeks later, in Toronto, I would hear him make the point again. "When I was diagnosed with ADHD in my early fifties, and then a couple of my kids were diagnosed, that seemed to prove it was a genetic disorder that's passed on through the DNA. But I never bought into that. And the reason I didn't is that I understood that the tuning out—which is the hallmark of ADHD—the dissociation from present-moment reality, is *not* a *disease,* inherited or otherwise. It's protection from pain or stress." The pain and stress, the trauma, of being alive, he added, is only growing, the need to tune out, to not pay attention, only becoming more urgent, more widespread.

The girl sitting next to me, undergraduate age, with a face full of piercings, had tears welling in her eyes. After his speech, Maté was swarmed with people wanting to talk with him one on one, wanting him to sign their copies of his books and, in the process, perhaps, absolve them of their burdensome histories. He interacted with every one of them.

When we finally began the drive back to Vancouver, where Maté had his final appearance of the day, it was nearly dinnertime. In the car, we passed a bag of almonds back and forth. It was past eight o'clock when we arrived at a five-star hotel near Vancouver's picturesque waterfront. A conference was under way in the plush hotel ballroom, filled with elected officials from the various Canadian provinces. Maté made his way to the stage. He was there to deliver some brief remarks on homelessness. When he called for questions, I was taken aback, though by then I shouldn't have been, that a tidily coiffed woman in a business suit was standing at the mic, already fighting back tears, ready to explain herself. Between sobs, her story spilled out. As I listened to her narrate, about a crime that had taken place in her neighborhood, I couldn't help but notice that at this point, nearly ten hours after I had first arrived on Maté's front porch, I had hit a kind of saturation point, a state of numb detachment. But Maté, from the stage, appeared as engaged as at any point in the day, leaning forward to ask the woman at the microphone for more details, more feelings. I was thinking about Maté's daily reality. This seventy-three-year-old man, whose first year of life, as a Jewish baby in Budapest, was steeped in extreme stress, his very survival in question, now led an existence devoted to other people's pain. He saw trauma all around him, which in and of itself attracted traumatized people to him, who sought understanding and compassion for the situations in which they found themselves.

In the context of all this trauma, Maté believes, our technology is the perfect decoy, the perfect prop, so we do not have to sit in silence and look at our pain. There is always Instagram or Twitter, an article to read, a text message to send, a cat video to Google. We do not have to face it, or understand that it's there. So there it stays.

In fact, Maté's view of our personal technology evolved over the course of the time I knew him. At first, he told me, this technology was neutral, like any technology. The issue is not about our phones themselves, but rather, how we use them. Later, he acknowledged the cumulative research suggested a different conclusion. Technology, with its persuasive design, is not what we call "neutral." It is pointed directly at our vulnerabilities. Indeed, Maté said, it is the kid riddled with ADHD symptoms who is most likely to disappear for hours into video games, into screen time. It seems, then, that the technologists of Silicon Valley have intuited—or accidentally stumbled upon—just how desperate we really are to escape.

And I was too. I was now desperate to escape this hotel ballroom, these testimonies. I knew this about myself by then: at a certain point in the night, in the lecture, in the week, I loved to flee, to retreat to my habits and my solitude. I always longed to take an early flight home. I thought of David Foster Wallace jetting out of Plum Village, out from under the auspices of Thich Nhat Hanh. Wanting to learn and change, perhaps, but not as prescribed. I waited as long as I could, then waved goodbye to Maté from the back of the room. For all I know, he stayed onstage for hours, listening to everyone's stories.

11

I was invested in a story of my life that went like this: My life was charmed. That included the difficult parts, the years of addiction, and, as well, the childhood stuff, the kinds of experiences that, if I were differently inclined, I might be compelled to talk about in a room full of strangers at a Gabor Maté event somewhere in Canada. But I wasn't. I didn't see my life or myself as broken, as suffused with pain I needed someone else's help to transcend. Even when in the midst of therapy for getting off the Adderall, the tone, the subtext, was, in a sense, entirely optimistic: I know I would be better off without this bottle of amphetamines.

Perhaps that was why, when I was with Maté, at his many and various events, I often found myself battling an intense urge to flee. It wasn't only in Vancouver—it had happened to me in Toronto too, where I had gone to attend his two-day-long "compassionate inquiry" workshop and where I had spent the entire first morning Googling flights back to New York. I was obsessing over what to do: Should I abort the compassionate inquiry experience in order to attend a party that night in Manhattan with my boyfriend, Josh? As the other attendees at Maté's event all eagerly, even desperately, shot their hands out for the mic, hoping to tell of their pain, I couldn't stop scrolling through Expedia.com. I writhed in indecision until well past lunch, when I officially couldn't make it home in time no matter what plane I caught. Only then could I finally commit to just being there.

Maté's central belief that it's our psychic pain that keeps us scattering ourselves to the winds, our trauma, our childhood shit, was, at that time, intriguing, startling even, but not always personally resonant. I liked this idea of Maté's without feeling awakened by it, without feeling even the possibility of it liberating me from the old tape of my own distractions, my own distractibility. I kept it at a distance. And then, right in the midst of all my attention research, quite unexpectedly, my own attention was violently captured by the most painful turn of events of my life: my seventy-nine-year-old father falling afoul of the Me Too movement. I watched, helplessly firsthand, as the force of the Internet's viral attention turned against my own family member.

This was December 2017. I had just come in from looking at apartments: Josh and I were planning to move in together soon after the New Year. I couldn't remember a happier, more peaceful time. Then I picked up my phone to hear my father, Jonathan Schwartz, say: "I have something to tell you."

"Tell me," I said. I was used to dramatic narratives arriving in phone calls from my father, who had made a career as a professional raconteur and DJ on WNYC, the New York affiliate of National Public Radio (NPR). Between songs, he wove detailed stories about Sinatra and Sondheim, George and Ira

Gershwin, Rodgers and Hammerstein, and other musical legends, many of whom he had known since he was born. His own
father, Arthur Schwartz, was a Broadway composer, who had
written the score, most famously, to *The Band Wagon:* songs
like "Dancing in the Dark" and "That's Entertainment!" My
father's childhood, therefore, was steeped in his father's music,
the music of Broadway from the 1920s through the '50s, the
music that comprises the Great American Songbook.

"Two weeks ago," he began, "I was in the bathroom at the
station. A friend of mine was at the urinal next to me. When
we were both finished, as I passed him to leave, I sang a little to
him—'All of Me'—and I kind of patted the rhythm of it on his
shoulders. Apparently, he repeated the story. A woman from
HR called me and told me I was now on probation and if I did
one more thing, if there was one complaint against me, I'd be
fired immediately."

In the weeks since the Me Too movement began, NPR had
been convulsed by revelations that both the editorial director,
Michael Oreskes, as well as John Hockenberry, who hosted the
show *The Takeaway,* had been left in place despite years of complaints against them. Garrison Keillor had also recently been
let go—the old-fashioned, avuncular persona at the heart of the
long-running show *A Prairie Home Companion.* Like many, I'd
taken those developments on faith, assuming that these three
men were all equally guilty, and equally deserving of thorough punishment. I was, after all, a youngish woman who
completely identified with the goals of Me Too, who cheered
through Ronan Farrow's epic reporting on Harvey Weinstein
in *The New Yorker,* who could recite a list of my own experiences with predatory, boundary-violating, and sometimes trau-
matizing men, who was in awe of the women stepping forward
into the public eye, forsaking their anonymity, risking their

futures, to say what it was that had happened to them. But I was also the daughter of a well-known man who had never been like the other dads, keenly aware of the ways in which his eccentricities—his radical informality, his disdain for bourgeois etiquette, his pleasure in playfulness, in pranks, in disrupting the corporate texture of life—the very traits that had helped to fuel the success of his half-century-long career, could blow up in his face. As my father described the events at the station, I pictured the canvas bags emblazoned with the WNYC logo that left-leaning New Yorkers carry all over the city, proof that they have pledged to support their station, proof that they are a certain kind of person. I felt terror for my father.

"Just tell me, is everything okay now?" I blurted out.

He said yes. He told me the "higher-ups" had convened a meeting that my father had attended. "This has been handled," one had told him. Her meaning, as my father took it, was: don't worry, this is behind us now. Someone there had even apologized to my father. But before the other could speak, my father, his voice brimming with hostility, made it clear to her he was outraged that an incident like this one could have galvanized such a significant response.

"Dad, are you kidding me? Do you not understand where we are as a country?" I was even more alarmed now, sitting straight up on my bed.

"You weren't there, you don't understand how nasty she was to me."

"I don't care how nasty she was—you just lost a chance to make her your ally," I said. I was nearly shouting by then. "You clearly have no idea how vulnerable you really are as a man in public life right now."

My father became defensive. "These have been the most harrowing two weeks of my life," he said, and got off the phone. The next morning, I woke up to this email:

Casey, when all the women appeared [and here, I knew my father was referring to the women who had been coming forward against Weinstein, Charlie Rose, Matt Lauer, among others, in recent months] I searched through my life. What I found was nothing but agreeable relations. It has never been my idea to go after someone, even for a kiss. If the signals were green I saw them as green. Same thing with red. Sex can't be a one way deal.

Please tell your brother what happened to me and what I said to one of the HR women, to which you objected.

I will take your advice to heart

Dad

I had already told my brother, out on the West Coast, the story. I had texted him almost as soon as my father told it to me. Of course, we were taking his narrative on faith: we had not been in the bathroom to witness the episode in question. But the story so perfectly encapsulated our father: the childlike playfulness, even, especially, in an off-color location such as the men's bathroom. The choice of song: my father had been spontaneously bursting into the opening lines of "All of Me" since before we could even remember. *All of me, Why not take all of me? Can't you see, I'm no good without you* . . . These were the lines we'd heard him belt out on any number of Manhattan sidewalks, in restaurants, during car rides, at baseball games, on telephone calls. It was his signature serenade, his way of saying (I'd always felt): don't forget the music. Yet the story he told me on the phone also contained his darker side: his temper, which, though rare, could flare up disastrously at the most inopportune times. Everything about this story was quintessentially my father.

I read his email, rolled my eyes, and went about my morning. I had just stepped on the treadmill at the gym when my phone rang: my mother. "Can you talk for a second?" Her voice sounded strange. I lowered the speed to walking pace. "An email has gone around to NPR employees that your father's been suspended." I hit stop and hung up the phone. Standing in the window, my back turned to all the people sweating on their various machines, I dialed my father's cell phone. His Sinatra ring tone was already a tragic detail in this unfolding story. "Darling," he answered. "Dad, is it true? Are you suspended?" "It's true." "Dad, what did you do?" I was crying. "What did you do?" "Nothing, darling. Nothing. I am racking my brain. I have no idea what this is about." He was speaking to me from the black town car that had been waiting for him on Vandam Street, outside WNYC, when he arrived at work that day. A station employee had been positioned in the lobby to intercept him and direct him first up to HR, where he was told that he was suspended, but not why. Then he was sent home, via town car.

The news hit Twitter and text messages from friends began pouring in. I love my friends deeply, but I resented their pity and ignored their messages. The only thing I wanted was their outrage. Did they not understand? *He doesn't know what he's accused of.* My father had been given no specifics about what it was that made his conduct inappropriate, such as what he had done, or who said he had done it. We would, in fact, learn nothing more for the next ten days, a stretch of time during which the reputation he had built as a presence on American radio for fifty years seemed to be entirely undone and replaced with a new one: sexual predator.

I couldn't help but compulsively check Twitter to clock the speed with which the mysterious allegations of "inappropriate conduct" had already morphed into a sordid verdict in the court of public opinion. I thanked god for small mercies: "Jonathan Schwartz" wasn't trending. But there were more than enough tweets on the subject of my father's suspension, and I read them all with a sickening sensation. "I am really relieved I'll never have to listen to Jonathan Schwartz play the same song over and over again and then ramble about the fucking Red Sox ever again," wrote one listener. Another: "If you ever been listening to NPR and heard Jonathan Schwartz lick his lips then you know he was capable of sexual harassment." "Not surprised about Jonathan Schwartz who played horribly offensive and insensitive song Everyone Ought to Have a Maid . . ." As I scrolled, I saw that the allegations against my father were already, inevitably, being characterized as "sexual misconduct," though WNYC had not called them that. Within hours, my father's name had been turned into a hashtag that signified everything odious about the male gender. Twitter had spoken.

I had gone through my whole life thus far, all thirty-five years of it, as the daughter of a somewhat well-known New Yorker, disliked by some, beloved by others. Now, in the space of one day, that had been turned inside out. My new reality appeared to be this: I was the daughter of a disgraced almost eighty-year-old, one of the distasteful casualties of this moment in time, a man on the wrong side of history.

That night, I rode the F train home to Brooklyn from my father's apartment, sending texts back and forth with a friend the whole way as we tried to figure out how to change my online identity. I had never particularly cared before that a simple search of my name led directly to this one-line Google bio: "Jonathan Schwartz's daughter." It was absurdly patriarchal, to be sure, when I could have just as accurately been described as, for example, an "American journalist," granted my own standing in the world by Google's vaunted algorithms. But now, my Internet tagline wasn't merely irritating: it had become a potential liability, it seemed to me. Would I see consequences in my own life? I did not fear an overt reaction but rather a subtle shift: a different kind of response when I emailed my editors about stories I wanted to write, a change in the way friends and acquaintances regarded me, a certain kind of untouchability encircling my name, the name I share with my father.

The days ticked by in a blur, the shock giving way to a deep, unshakeable sadness. I wasn't able to do my work on attention. Instead, I was forced to pay attention to my father's catastrophe and how it was playing out, hour to hour, both privately and publicly. For the first time in my life, I felt that I had no control over where or how to direct my thoughts. Instead, I alternated between numbness, fury, and grief. I was terrified of my own sadness and fought against it, sending emails to people I cared about, nibbling an old Ritalin I still kept in my drawer, taking epic walks through freezing Brooklyn. My father, I knew, was sitting in his Midtown apartment, shattered, sending his own plaintive emails to friends, sometimes answering his phone. When we spoke, he was semi-coherent, in a fog of pain and confusion.

Ten days after his suspension, my father went to a law firm in Midtown, where the outside investigator WNYC had hired would ask him a series of questions about his alleged behavior. The meeting began at 2:00 p.m. His lawyer had warned him to expect the conversation to take well over an hour, maybe two. At 2:45, therefore, I was surprised to receive a text from his lawyer: "He did great. He will call you."

That was a Friday. On the following Thursday, my father was fired. He still didn't understand why.

It seemed to me that at the core of Me Too was this simple, obvious truth: women's experiences must be taken seriously, as seriously as men's. But how can we claim to value the sanctity of a woman's life, to say nothing of her civil rights, if we appeared willing to disregard those of a man? If we were happy to say, for example, that men should lose their jobs, their names, and their futures without the ability to defend themselves and without, in some cases, including my father's, full knowledge of the accusations against them?

But, of course, this isn't about gender—or it shouldn't be. It's about seeking justice, regardless of gender. Until I saw it firsthand, I hadn't understood that for many of these accused, in this moment, due process had been abandoned. I think that was the fact that most broke my heart.

A few months later, WNYC would finalize its offer of a settlement with my father. It came with a nondisclosure agreement he had to sign in exchange for the money. I got back on the phone with my father's lawyer to understand the implications of this NDA, of what I could and could not say if I did choose to say anything.

As a journalist, my first instinct was to tell my story, the story of what my family had gone through. But for the first time in my career, I was afraid. There seemed to be no room to offer anything like a complicated Me Too narrative without being savaged on social media, and by my very own demographic: young, left-wing, mostly women, who, like me, support the larger goals of Me Too. I didn't want to be here, but here I was, forced by my father's experience into a consciousness that divided me from many of my contemporaries.

And it was everywhere. Or that's how it felt to me. A cascade of men I knew, the husbands and fathers of friends and acquaintances, also had their day in the pages of *The New York Times*. Every Twitter thread I read, there it was. The anger. The relish in toppling men. An old fling of mine came to town and we met for a drink. He knew what had happened to my father but told me, quite sternly, this was the price of revolution. He seemed miffed I didn't see it this way, then, anger mounting, told me his mother's career had been curtailed by harassment in the workplace, as had those of so many women, and that's what Me Too was all about, righting that wrong. If my father and others like him were collateral damage, that's how it was and how it should be. I couldn't help but marvel that it was this man in particular who was explaining Me Too to me, this man who had once wrapped both hands around my upper thigh, to let me know he was measuring, and I wasn't measuring up.

I turned down two different offers to write about what had happened. I concluded that I wasn't tough enough, tough like the small band of journalists—nearly all of them women—who had written about the movement with less-than-unconditional support for its methods. They had been blasted on social media with such vitriol that it had shaken me. I surmised that the popular slogan "Believe Women" in fact applied only to certain women, telling certain stories.

I knew that whatever I wrote, I'd be seen as biased, blind, or possibly worse. I also knew that my story could inspire unknown accusers out of the woodwork, someone else who had somewhere along the line been offended by my father and now had a damning new label to apply to him.

For the fact was my father's case, like every case, was not perfectly black and white. Ultimately, we would hear there were some complaints against him but not of what they comprised or exactly when they were made. We heard a rumor that one involved his complimenting a coworker's haircut. One coworker stated in a blog post that he'd been "inappropriate" but not the "least bit traumatic." Another rumor had it that he had made an off-color comment about his boss. I came to believe that WNYC saw him as ill-suited to the new rules of Me Too, un-coachable, a man nearing eighty who couldn't be made new. My father, on the other hand, according to the NDA he eventually signed, is allowed to say that he wasn't fired for reasons of sexual misconduct.

It was quitting time when I arrived in Mountain View. Months had passed, Christmas and everything that had come with it receding into the background, somehow. My mind had shifted back to my work, my subject. My attention had returned to attention. At the invitation of a new friend, I had come to Google's campus. I wanted to see the company that had erected the very infrastructure of our attention economy.

I was surprised by how quiet it was. A long line of buses waited patiently outside one of the squat, unremarkable office buildings dotting the campus. I didn't know there was a strict prohibition on photography, and I began snapping away at the picturesque multicolored bikes provided for Googlers to traverse their environs. This was what I was doing when the doors opened and workers began streaming out of their various buildings, making their way toward the buses that would transport them home to San Francisco. Many wore thick, noise-canceling headphones and walked alone, glancing at me strangely as I continued to take my photos, but saying nothing.

As my host and I walked across the tidy lawns separating the squat buildings, it occurred to me to bring up another question altogether. "Could we stop by whatever office is in charge of writing the bios?" I'd like to have mine changed, I explained. I was still identified as "Jonathan Schwartz's daughter."

"Oh, that would be really difficult," he told me. "There's no office for that. It's more like our algorithms recognize that as the primary fact about you. It's all based on page views."

"So, if I were to write about my father, I would actually make that association much worse?" I asked him.

"Pretty much," he said, shrugging sympathetically.

The way I saw things by then had grown a little more detached. I had come to feel that I had witnessed an Internet-specific phenomenon, a case study from the pages of Jon Ronson's *So You've Been Publicly Shamed.* My father, like many other men, had been declared guilty by strangers on the Internet before they knew of what he was accused. The Twitter conversation had spread instantly, in the absence of facts, fueled by an enormous amount of collective emotion, of righteousness, of denouncement, of rage.

There were scientists studying exactly this phenomenon: how moral outrage spreads online. I called one of them, Molly Crockett, a slightly reserved, extremely accomplished thirty-five-year-old with her own lab at Yale. Crockett, a neuroscientist, studies morality and moral transformation. I wanted to talk to her about attention, I said, about the specific ways that Internet platforms seize and keep our attention.

"One of the things that reliably captures our attention is anything having to do with morality," she said. "Separating who's a good guy from who's a bad guy is probably the most important thing our brains do, because being able to figure out who our friends and enemies are is pretty much one of the most important things for our survival. So it makes sense that our brains would have evolved to devote a lot of resources to solving that problem.

"Moral content, especially moral content that triggers emotion, which is a sign of importance—that's going to grab our attention. If you build a technological system that selects content on its ability to grab our attention, you're going to disproportionately be showing people content that pushes their moral buttons.

"One potential unintended consequence of all of this is that we are constantly bombarded with outrage-triggering content—and it could reduce our ability to separate signal from noise, and ultimately break down our ability to sort out which problems really need our attention, and which are superficial button pressing."

She added, somewhat offhandedly, that Me Too had made her for the first time believe that something good could come from the wildfire spread of digital outrage. At this, I said nothing. I didn't tell her that I don't see it in precisely those terms. I didn't tell her I was asking as much as a daughter as a reporter. Infinitely easier to be the reporter, get the quote, hang up the phone.

12

It was warm and salty, chalky and bittersweet. It tasted like the blood of some old, old thing.

—TERENCE McKENNA

January, just. For the last month, I'd been living in crisis mode, immersed in the wreckage of my father's situation. This was before Google, before detachment. I was still raw, rocked, ranting at parties, crying on sidewalks. Calling my father every day, attempting to permeate the fog and the sadness in his voice, attempting to process what had happened to him with such suddenness, and such finality. I was so wrapped up in our family drama I had barely had time to contemplate my upcoming trip to the equator. And now that it was upon me, I had serious misgivings about getting on the plane.

When I had made the first phone call, to a high-end ayahuasca retreat in Central America, I knew nothing of what December held in store. All I knew when I dialed that number a few days before Thanksgiving was that in some sense, this trip was preordained, by my acquaintance with Gabor Maté, and with David, my ex from the Adderall days, before him.

My call was answered by an automated recording, which, in female British robot tones, thanked me for dialing this "life enhancement center." Making the call from my office in far-away Brooklyn, I found the robot's message somewhat chilling, as if I might soon be entering a Charlie Kaufman movie, one that would require me to turn over the contents of my memory for professional intervention. At that time, I did not wish to experiment directly with ayahuasca, the powerful psychedelic tea made from the *Banisteriopsis caapi* vine, native to the Amazon. Indeed, I was quite frightened of the substance, which can induce hours of uncontrollable vomiting, shitting, and powerful, all-consuming hallucinations. Rather, I was calling as a reporter: Gabor Maté was scheduled to spend a week at this particular retreat as a guest speaker, helping the attendees to "integrate" their nightly ayahuasca sessions.

Maté first tried ayahuasca about a decade ago, when his book *In the Realm of Hungry Ghosts* came out, and everyone started asking him what he knew about treating addiction with plant medicine. I had heard him tell the story several times. I'd heard him explain how "irritating" it was to be asked about ayahuasca, about which he knew nothing, rather than the four hundred–plus pages of material he'd spent years assiduously research-ing and compiling for his addiction magnum opus. And yet, enough people asked him about it that he finally decided to try it for himself.

"When I did try it, I got it right away," he told me. "I always knew that healing from trauma is possible for everybody and there are lots of great modalities that have nothing to do with psychedelics. But nothing expedites healing as well as psyche-delics do."

I had asked Maté, months before, if he believed there was

a connection between our technology-saturated lives and the recent resurgence of interest in psychedelic drugs, including ayahuasca. Yes, he said. Unequivocally.

"Psychedelics have the capacity to bring people very much into the present moment. Where they're attending to not what's going on outside themselves, but to what's going on inside," he explained.

"Technology, instead of uniting people, actually separates them. It creates more alienation. It creates more addiction. So that actually Facebook doesn't pull people together, it disconnects them. Technology is just another part of the social pattern that drives alienation that we then need to find a solution for. Hence psychedelics."

Maté had said this over lunch in a tiny sushi place in Vancouver. As he spoke, I had the thought it was somewhat ironic that it was this problematic technology that also connects people with the psychedelic experiences they seek, for the simple reason that, with the Internet, it has become infinitely easier to figure out how and where to do drugs that are not yet legal and may never be.

I had committed to go, in large part because I wanted to see this side of Maté's working life. But the truth was, however alluring "high-end retreat" and "Central America" might be expected to sound to a frozen New Yorker in January, I was anxious about it. As my departure date approached, I became increasingly unhappy about my decision; the night before my flight, I came close to canceling altogether. I was channeling all my anxiety and discomfort into one looming obsession: the Zika virus. Why was I, with hopes of having a kid at some point in the nearish future, flying into the sticky equatorial regions, depicted on the Centers for Disease Control website as solid purple with Zika risk? But I knew too that beyond my Zika anxiety lay the greater fear of the role I was going to play once there: the watcher, the solo sober voyeur in the group's midst, looking on from the sidelines as everyone around me embarked on intensely personal, nightly, hallucinatory journeys. Because I was now officially resigned to the periphery: due to the crisis that had rocked my family only four weeks before, I hadn't been able to get off the antidepressants I was prescribed—the same Wellbutrin given to me nearly a decade before to help get me off the Adderall. They were the last vestiges of the chemical speediness I had so adored from age eighteen to thirty, my last little prescription thrill. But, according to the medical thinking that governed the policy at the retreat to which I was headed, one must not mix antidepressants and ayahuasca. Therefore, I did not have the option of trying the plant medicine myself, even if I wanted to, which, at that point in time, I absolutely did not. After placing several panicked midnight phone calls to friends and family, asking them all what they thought I should do and finding no consensus, I duly woke up at sunrise and dragged my suitcase to JFK. It was the first Sunday of the new year.

In my seat on the plane, I opened the short book written by the retreat's founder. Pamphlet size, it looked about one step up from self-published. The book told Gianni's story: how he had been rich from business ventures from a young age, and also addicted to booze, drugs, and sex. How he cheated on his wife, vanished from family life at will, and once passed out with a needle full of tranquilizer sticking out of his vein in front of his young son. He was also intensely depressed, angry, and empty. He'd done rehab and years of therapy, but none of it had really helped him. By luck, a woman he vaguely knew told him to try plant medicine. Out of desperation, he flew to Central America, still drunk upon arrival from the bender he'd gone on at the airport. But after one session, he wrote, his life transformed. The vices that had captivated his mind for decades lost their power, their electrical charge. All he could see now were the years of damage he had done, all the urgent opportunities to repair.

Six years later, he was the owner of a well-known ayahuasca retreat, divested of his former business interests—including a chain of strip clubs he had planned to open in airports around the country—living most of the time in Central America so he could work with the groups that came through each week, helping each one to find what they came all this way for: their own radical transformation. I read his short book quickly, then leaned back and shut my eyes. I didn't know what to expect.

At baggage claim, I slathered on my heavy-duty mosquito repellent and headed out into the humid sunshine. A shuttle driver was waiting on the curb, holding up a sign with the name of the retreat. He told me a couple of others from my flight would be along shortly. I had been trying to predict who else on the plane might be heading to my same destination. At the gate in New York, I had gone so far as to ask a spritely, sparkly eyed man with a Brooklyn-approved handlebar mustache and fashionable hat if he was on his way to a week of ayahuasca. "Oh dear, no, most definitely not!" he had told me. He looked vaguely worried for me. I would never have picked the woman who did emerge into the roasting afternoon a few minutes after me. She appeared to be close to my own age, with a thick New York accent and a wistful, apologetic demeanor. We introduced ourselves and stood near the shuttle driver and his sign. As we waited there, an older woman with the brown skin of the region and long gray pigtail braids, a dour expression on her face, approached us.

"Are you prepared?" she said. She stared at us. "Are you?"

We said nothing. She continued. "I'm a shaman. Where you're going, it's a factory."

I understood then that her dour expression was likely connected to the tensions stirred up by the ayahuasca tourist industry, a relatively new economy in developing Central and South American countries. The existence of the well-known, high-end retreat to which we were headed had taken the ayahuasca economy to a new level, introducing four-star tourism where there had been huts, tents, and improvised cabins. I'd been assured, for example, that there was a treadmill on the premises. A team of masseurs. And a doctor.

Finally, Lizzy, my new companion, broke the loaded silence. "Yes," she said. "I'm ready." The shaman just squinted back with her joyless face. The shuttle driver signaled to us to follow him to the parking lot. I started walking but sensed that Lizzy wasn't keeping pace. When I turned back, I saw that the two women were still in front of the airport entrance, holding each other in a tight embrace.

The history of ayahuasca in the North American consciousness was for a long time one of obscurity, shrouded in rumors and, most of all, rooted in near total inaccessibility. In the early 1950s, the writer William Burroughs, burdened by his circumstances (namely, his sexuality, his heroin addiction, and the fact that he had accidentally shot and killed his wife), left his home in Mexico City and came south, searching for the mythical "yagé" vine he had begun to hear about here and there. But for Burroughs, at that time, it was not a simple matter of booking a plane ticket and turning up. Instead, in 1953, he embarked on an arduous, months-long expedition through South America, paying off local guides, getting robbed, trekking through jungles in a pith helmet, being stranded in remote outposts for days at a time, waiting for the river to subside so he could proceed by canoe to where he had heard the shamans were: sometimes rightly, sometimes not. The book that resulted from all this, *The Yage Letters,* is a record of his correspondence with Allen Ginsberg throughout his attempts to find ayahuasca. "I must go," he wrote to Ginsberg on the eve of his departure. "I must find the yage."

Arriving at the retreat where I would spend the next week, it became clear that many of the people there—and there were roughly eighty of us—felt the same undeniable pull toward the yagé that Burroughs had expressed more than half a century before. On our first evening in camp, we congregated in the yoga pavilion, a comfortable, pristine, glassed-in structure, with removable foam plastic flooring (I would soon understand why) and air-conditioning. This was where the ayahuasca ceremonies would be held, beginning the following night. The camp itself, a gated compound, could have been any other nice holiday destination, the clean, spare rooms spread out around the property, and at the middle, a pool, and a poolside café serving coconut water and perpetually refreshed supplies of dried guava and pineapple. In the yoga pavilion, lounging on mats and plush blankets, we were asked to state our intentions in coming here. I jotted down the various replies in my notebook: "I'm here for radical healing." "To love life again." "To meet my own soul." "It's time to make changes." Gabor, two mats down from me, in beige cargo shorts, went before I did. "I'm here to learn," he said. His wife, Rae, who was traveling with him, pixie-like, with twinkling eyes behind glasses, made the same response. I lamely echoed them. I felt as if I were saying: I'm here to learn, but *not* to change.

I knew that if my old friend David were here, my ex from

the Adderall days, he would have a totally different approach to mine. David's years of ayahuasca had led him to this realization: "I carry my grandmother's pain from the Holocaust." David's own father had been born in France, in hiding, in 1944, the same year as Gabor Maté, to the same atmosphere of extreme peril and stress. It took David more than thirty years to realize he was walking around not only with his father's unresolved grief and trauma, but also, in fact, with his grandmother's. And, actually, his cure was a feat of attention: letting himself see and feel, to the fullest possible extent, the experience of this legacy.

We were seated in the central pavilion for this exchange, where the four ayahuasca ceremonies would take place, beginning the following night. The group was in some sense surprising to me: by a rough estimate, there appeared to be more people in their fifties and sixties than in their twenties and thirties. I would think of this fact later, reading Michael Pollan's masterwork on psychedelic science, *How to Change Your Mind*. Carl Jung wrote that it is people in middle age who need an "experience of the numinous" to navigate the next years of their lives, more so than people in youth and early adulthood. Reflecting on Jung's words, Pollan writes, "I've begun to wonder if perhaps these remarkable molecules might be wasted on the young, that they may have more to offer us later in life, after the cement of our mental habits and everyday behaviors has set."

Most people around me were American, but a handful had traveled much longer distances: from England, Australia, Austria, and Portugal. We even had a handsome Iranian musician in our midst. And, of course, because Gabor Maté was in residence this week, a flock of Canadians had come along too. Many people, in fact, were there specifically because of their interest in Maté's work and the opportunity this afforded to be with him in such close quarters. One of the first things I had learned about

Lizzy at the airport was that she was a Maté devotee, a follower of his work for years; she had even flown to London once, just to see him speak.

I was drawn to a stunning young New Yorker, a modern dancer. She had come here, she said, "to liberate myself." Raised by a single mother in economic stress, in a town where eighth-graders regularly got pregnant, she had turned her life into a success story, only to feel that she couldn't enjoy it or even fully inhabit it. Everyone, it seemed, had a kind of existential urgency to their reasons for being there. For most, if not all of us, this week was a high-stakes endeavor in the tropical sunshine.

"This isn't a week for the meek," Gianni, the charismatic owner, said to us all, to begin day number one. "This is super, super hard. By Wednesday a lot of you are going to want to leave. Those fences you saw—they ain't there to keep out the Indians."

"The Indian is right here," said a young Indian-Canadian woman sitting behind me. Gianni smiled his earnest, ever-so-slightly shy, childlike smile and simply continued.

He told us his story, which I knew from having read his short book, now with more detail: the violent childhood, the end of his education at sixteen years old, his first million dollars before the age of thirty. It was, I now understood, a kind of stump speech, one that he delivered every Monday morning, to the week's fresh recruits. Yet, in my experience of it, there was nothing canned about the rendition. He spoke from the heart about the booze, the drugs, the women that he'd consumed throughout his marriage. And then the desperation that prompted him onto a plane to Central America for his first encounter with plant medicine. He recalled that first night on psychedelics in vivid detail, laying out his "trip to the moon" as if providing us with a travelogue, one with a perfect interior logic that didn't need much explanation. "The moon explained to me that everybody, between when they're conceived and five years old, has a life occurrence that causes them to leave their soul and become someone else. *Everybody*," he said. "And she called it 'the split.' She said, 'You're all designed to split.'" As he spoke, he was diagramming the moon's message on the whiteboard behind him. "She said, once this split happens, that all disease, all disorder, all addiction comes from this loss."

I glanced around the room. The assembled group was rapt, nodding. I gathered that they knew exactly what was meant by "the split." Gianni was diagramming the split on the whiteboard, drawing a shape like an ankh, gesturing to its different components. "The moon told me that pre-split, you only want four things: to love, to be loved, to have a sense of community, and to have fun. After the split, you have another priority: to be right." The whole point, the whole reason for coming down for a week of ayahuasca, was to heal the split, "to merge back with your soul," "to become the little girl or boy you were meant to be." This was what Gianni meant when he referred, as he often would in the days ahead, to "the miracle." "Ninety-three percent of all visitors get their miracle," he was assuring us now. "And we're working on getting that number higher."

While he spoke, he picked up a thick, bound manuscript of pages lying on the table beside him. He explained that this was a printout of every question he'd asked the moon since that first night he'd met her and every answer she'd given him. The dialogue was remarkably practical. It included such exchanges as:

Q: Am I supposed to be monogamous?
A: To be really happy, you should be with just one person.
Q: How can I stop texting women?

A: Texting requires moving your fingers. Doing nothing requires nothing. Doing nothing is easier!

Q: Where are the records of my life stored?

A: They are stored in your soul, not your mind.

But getting to these answers, getting the promised miracle, was not going to be easy. He warned us there was going to be, first of all, excretion of all kinds: crying, vomiting, shitting. In fact, it was important to wear loose pants, easily removed, to the ceremony tonight. "Speed matters," Gianni said. "Seconds matter." Furthermore, each person would have their own plastic bucket and it was imperative, when racing to the bathroom, to bring the bucket with you, in case you threw up on the way. The sudden movement could often bring on the retching. "And when you throw up, ask the bucket, what *was* that?" Gianni advised. "See what it tells you."

"The medicine always wins. It will always break you down," he said. "Because if it's done right, it will call into question everything you've ever thought or believed."

That afternoon, we gathered in the yoga pavilion for Maté's first seminar. A lazy after-lunch atmosphere pervaded the sunshine-filled space; barefoot, we sprawled out on the plastic foam floor. "'Attention' and 'intention'—what do those words come from? Both come from the word *tenere,* which means to stretch. So when you're paying someone attention, you're stretching yourself toward themselves. With intention, you are stretching yourself toward some inner purpose. What is it that you're committed to extending yourself toward, internally?"

Maté called for questions, volunteers. At length, a woman

with close-cropped hair and a warm, maternal quality raised her hand.

"I feel that I'm not good enough," she said into the mic.

"That's an opinion, it's not a feeling. So how do you *feel* when you're not good enough?" Maté pressed her.

"I feel small."

"Feeling small is not a feeling. What is the actual feeling?"

She tried a few more answers.

"Inferior?"

"That's not a feeling, that's an opinion," he said.

"Can I say invisible?"

"You can, but it would not be accurate."

Finally, he provided the answer he was looking for: "Shame."

"Yeah, yeah. Definitely," she said.

"Please tell me about your childhood."

"There were five children in our family," she said. "I grew up being trained to be a mother to my brothers. My mom was a nice human being, but I think I didn't have my childhood, maybe? I never had my childhood. I was raising my brothers."

"At what age did you start raising your brothers?"

"Six."

"Your parents were together?"

"Yes—they are still together."

"Were they happy?"

"Very happy," she said. "Well, mostly."

"Tell me about the mostly."

"Well, I found out later in life that actually my dad had never been faithful to my mom."

"Okay, so when you were growing up, your father was sleeping with other women."

"Lots."

"Lots. And your mother knew?"

"She did. But she never said anything about it."

"How do you think she felt about it?"

"Crushed."

"Looking back now, from the adult point of view, did you sense that that was on her mind?"

"Oh, absolutely, yes."

"That's why you're not good enough. Because you couldn't fix it for her. You were not just a mother to your brothers—you were a mother to your mother, as well."

As he finished speaking these words, she burst into tears, inhaling in squeaky convulsions, head bowed into her arms. "Now I finally understand," she said after a moment or two, "where all of this comes from."

I was not, by now, surprised by any display of emotion evoked in dialogue with Gabor Maté. It was here just as it had been in Vancouver, in Toronto, and in Los Angeles, where I had seen Maté work with audiences at a spiffy tech-crowd conference called Summit. In every room, in every group, there were, it became clear, roiling waves of pain just beneath the surface— and as well, even more so, there was the need to engage with it, express it, unload it. Indeed, the instinct toward healing now appeared to me as a gravitational force in its own right, pulling people outside themselves, grasping for something, anything, that might be their cure.

At dusk, we reconvened in the yoga pavilion, nervously waiting for the first night's ceremony. The shaman, a white guy from New Jersey with a sweet face and a high-pitched giggle, who looked thirty but would prove to be fifty-three, had already paced the periphery, waving smoking sage in preparation. Next to his cushioned seat, six large glass bottles were arranged in a perfect row, a thick reddish-brown liquid inside, like hot sauce. We lined up in groups, solemnly, quietly, and approached the shaman for our dose. Mine was a special homeopathic concoction, the essence of the ayahuasca vine distilled down to the millionth degree, which he sprayed into my mouth like Binaca. The dose was so small it would not interfere with my prescription pills. I returned to my seat at the outermost edge of things, trying to savor the bitter plant flavor suffusing my tongue. I had chosen a perch on the outside wing, which had no walls, and from where I would have a perfect view of the night sky and its brilliant, undiluted stars.

In the minutes before the ceremony had begun, Maté had come around to wish everyone a good journey, joining certain people for a brief cross-legged conversation on their mattress. Maté had explained his investment in ayahuasca at length to me, months before. "When we disconnect, we substitute a lot of coping mechanisms. Those coping mechanisms become identified as our personality, our persona, we identify with them. We start to think we are those mechanisms," he said. "The plant actually relaxes the hold of the inauthentic persona of the mind and you see what's underneath it. What people find underneath it can be very beautiful or very difficult. They find underneath it tremendous rage, tremendous fear, terror, in fact. Then they may think: this is the plant doing this to me. But in fact it's not the plant doing it to them, it's what they've carried in them all their lives, they just didn't know it. But the other thing they can find is real peace, real love, real presence, which is the self they disconnected from in the first place. So people have an opportunity to revisit what they've been afraid to experience all their lives, what they've been running from all their lives. They get to experience who they were before they ran." Now, having completed his round of the room, he retired into himself on his own bed, eyes closed, face a mask of concentrated repose as he waited for the ayahuasca he'd drunk to take effect.

It didn't take long before the retching began. From where I sat, through the darkness, I could see the figure of the first woman to vomit. The sounds she was making did not line up with vomiting as I knew it. These noises seemed to come from a deeper, more primal place, like an animal in the woods, expelling poison berries, fighting for its life. I couldn't help but think of an exorcism. After a while, one of the staff members, a lovely young woman with blond and pink braids and an earth mother disposition, came over to wave burning sage around the woman as she purged, and sing to her, quietly, what sounded like a blessing. Music played softly from speakers set up around the pavilion, the songs in Spanish. I disappeared into a trance, staring at the starlight.

I was struggling with tremendous regret that I couldn't have this experience myself. Just six weeks before, the idea of trying ayahuasca had filled me with dread and aversion; now, I was envious of everyone around me who would understand first-hand what this experience consisted of, what exactly was the mechanism of change. All I could do was look on from the sidelines, relegated to my nonparticipant status because of my Wellbutrin pills, which I didn't even need. Suddenly, I heard a voice, with crystalline clarity, speak to me with a simple directive.

"Get off the antidepressants *now*," it said. The voice was genderless, but unequivocal.

I looked up at the stars.

All right, I thought. I will.

The next morning I woke up early and headed to the gym, feeling a bit absurd about it. Everyone else was still in bed recovering from a night of profound visions and revelations. In a sense, I had had one too. I knew it was against medical advice to stop the Wellbutrin abruptly instead of more gradually discontinuing it. But, uncharacteristically, I didn't waver.

I wandered around in the tropical sunshine, unsure of what to do with myself. It was day two. I had a pit of unease in my stomach, a strange, unshakable paranoia that by the end of the week, the group, united in its impenetrable ayahuasca intimacy, would turn on me, the watcher, the judger. It was, I recognize now, the kind of thinking born of isolation in a gated compound, yet that day it consumed me, and by the time 6:00 p.m. came, and people began convening for that night's ceremony, I decided I couldn't bring myself to attend, and went down to dinner at the restaurant instead. For most, the evening meal was not an option: no food after 2:00 p.m. if you planned to drink the medicine.

I found Gabor, his wife, Rae, and four staff members already gathered around a table in the restaurant. Gabor had drunk the ayahuasca the night before, a small dose of it, but was sitting out tonight's proceedings. I had chosen to confide in Gabor, I'm not entirely sure why, about the situation with my father. On our very first night in residence, I had pulled him aside. "Do you know what's been going on with my father?" I asked him, a question that speaks to the state of mind I was in that week, that month. I was walking the world in a state of self-involved paranoia, assuming that everyone knew, just as Google knew, which father's daughter I was, and what kind of person he was now presumed to be.

It turned out Maté knew neither of these things, but just as I was explaining—"on WNYC for twenty years and now he's been fired for Me Too accusations"—he cut me off. "It doesn't matter what he's done," he told me, although it did, it mattered terribly. What could possibly matter more? "The only thing that matters is how you feel about it," he said. Perhaps another person would have found great liberation in Maté's message. As it happened, I did not.

"How are you finding the week?" he asked me now, as I took a seat at the dinner table.

"It's interesting," I said.

There was a loaded pause.

"There's a word you use a lot," he said. " 'Interesting.' I want to read you a quote about people who use the word 'interesting.' " He pulled out his phone and began searching for the saved quotation. By now, all five people at the table were silent, watching my exchange with Maté.

" 'Interesting' means you can keep your distance, play around with ideas and concepts in your mind, agree or disagree," Maté read to me. Later, I would learn he was quoting Eckhart Tolle. He looked up to add his own point: "But it never leads to a change in consciousness."

"Can I say more? Is that okay?" he asked, just as I had heard him ask the people he dialogued with in his trauma seminars.

"By all means, go ahead," I said.

"I think you like to stay detached, and then you rationalize it by saying you're a journalist. I can see you rationalizing ways of staying fairly disengaged."

As the five other people at the table stared at us, I felt a red-hot defiance leap up inside me. The last thing I experience myself to be, in my life, is disengaged. If anything, I could often do with a great deal more detachment. "In fairness, detachment is an essential part of journalistic training," I heard myself saying, cringing at my own pretentiousness.

"Maybe, maybe," he continued. "Or maybe this week is a good opportunity for you to get curious about your own detachment."

I paused. "Do you ever wonder if there's a risk of over-pathologizing the people you're talking to?" I asked now. I was somewhat losing my cool, I knew. I also knew what was provoking me: Maté's implicit claim of omniscience, of knowing me better than I knew myself. "The fact is, I'm not here because my life needs drastic renovations."

"Do you hear me saying you are?" he asked.

"I think it's in your subtext."

"Oh, so you experience me as having a subtext?"

Throughout this exchange, monstrous locusts, about eight inches long, were flying like small bats around the little outdoor café, missing faces and heads by mere centimeters, careening half blind into any surfaces they happened to approach. Rumor had it that their legs were sharp and mildly poisonous. Throughout the meal, Gabor's wife and I would scream and duck under the table whenever a nearby locust took flight. Gabor, sitting between us, didn't flinch. Finally, we gave up and ran to our rooms. Or was that just me? I didn't stop to find out. Huddled under a thin white blanket as my air conditioner blasted away the natural environment, I looked up flights back to the United States, fantasizing about an early departure. I didn't know if I could handle the rest of the week: the flying locusts, the laser beam of Gabor Maté, the withdrawal from ten years of antidepressant medication, or the building destabilization I felt like a brewing tropical storm, the psychological humidity already thick in the air.

It was the next morning at breakfast that the crying began. "Last night, I saw the suffering of all humanity, and it is *endless*," one woman from the Pacific Northwest told me, over thick green spirulina smoothies. "I saw all my ancestors. I saw each one of them in so much pain." Next to her, a beautiful blonde from the Midwest was quiet for a while, listening.

Finally, she told us what her own night had brought. "I saw my husband in a casket." This was Kimberly, who, in her late fifties, mother of three, looked ten years younger, with radiant skin and perfect red toenails. She began sobbing out the story of her marriage to an alcoholic, the decades she'd devoted to being his caretaker, her own "unsupported life." And for the last two nights, the ayahuasca had relentlessly shown her—as if she didn't already know—his imminent demise. She was embarrassed by her own outburst, and I understood how uncharacteristic it must have been for her to reveal herself in this way.

I was wondering about a woman who'd come here from England. In her sixties now, she'd lost her leg to an accident in London decades before. I had seen her in a deep sleep the afternoon before, passed out on a sofa in the yoga pavilion while the rest of us listened to Maté's daily lecture. This was Franny. When I found her on Wednesday, I stopped to ask how she was. "Not good," she said, tears pooling in her eyes, spilling out on her cheeks. "I'm in pain, terrible pain. I've been asleep for the last twenty hours. I couldn't go to the ceremony last night. And I don't think I'll be able to make it tonight. I don't know if I can do that to my body. Isn't this the body saying no? I think my body is saying *no*." Her tears were flowing continuously now. Yet that night, back in the yoga pavilion come sunset, lying on my appointed mattress on the edge of the proceedings, I looked up just in time to see Franny approach the shaman and throw down the little glass of ayahuasca like a bracing shot of whiskey. The next morning, she arrived at the breakfast table wearing hot pink lipstick. She was beaming.

Not everyone had had that kind of a night. The woman I had lain next to had clearly been suffering. It had started with twitching. Little twitches, a jerking of an arm, then a leg; they soon became full-body events, like she was trying to brush a million tropical bugs off her skin. When the sounds of retching started around us, she yanked the blanket above her head. Then she sat up, throwing off the blanket, and began forcefully flailing her limbs in the air, like she was trying to eliminate whatever troubled her about them, perhaps the limbs themselves. In the dark, she turned to look at me. She knew that I wasn't on the ayahuasca, only the mild homeopathic dose they kept for those not partaking. I couldn't help but feel that my unaligned presence was contributing to her problems. After awhile, I slipped away, walking back to my room, careful to avoid the dreadful locusts that lurked on the pathways. The next morning, when she appeared at breakfast, her face was splotchy and red, her dissatisfaction apparent. The fact that her boyfriend, a delicate-looking, mild-mannered man, had, by contrast, "gotten his miracle" on the very first night didn't seem to help matters much.

By day, we were busy: there was yoga; there were seminars ("The answer is YOU," among other subjects); there were massages; there were colonics. But most of all, there was conversation: from sunrise until ceremony, people sat in clusters and talked in intensely personal detail about their lives and about what the ayahuasca was revealing to them. Phones were not banned but seemed to naturally recede to the periphery. What I was observing around me was the most basic, low-tech kind of human exchange. And the hunger for it was unmistakable.

By Friday, I could see the arc of change all around me: personalities had melted down and opened up. The female doctor who, in our first days together, had rigidly shut down my attempt at engagement, not even looking up once from her plate of food when her lunch companion started choking, was now chatty and extroverted. The beautiful dancer, her skin visibly glowing with a new level of radiance, exuded peace and confidence. "I'm a fairy *and* a tiger," she told me, at the final dinner. "That's what the medicine told me. I'm incredible. I can't believe I ever doubted that." Kimberly, the midwesterner whose alcoholic husband, back at home, had in fact landed in the ER while she was in an ayahuasca ceremony, seemed beatific. "I've made peace with it," she told me. "Whatever comes, I'm okay."

Almost everyone, it appeared, had gotten their miracle. Except me, of course. And Gabor. "I've never experienced that 'merger,'" he had told me.

"That's not so surprising," his wife, Rae, had replied. "You know, Gabor, you really don't seem very happy." She apparently meant this as a neutral observation, and Gabor, nodding, seemed to take it as one.

Before I left, Gianni pulled me aside. "Come back here. Come back here for free," he said. "Come back when you can drink the medicine. You won't even need that much—you're so ready for it." I had told Gianni about what had happened with my father the month before. I wasn't sure if this was what he was referring to, or something deeper, more fundamental, but I was moved by his sincerity. I sensed he wouldn't have been able to extend himself in this way to me if not for the change that had come through his life, six years before. I said I would think about it. But even in that moment, I knew I probably wouldn't be back. After all, there was still the Zika factor: it was as good an alibi as any. I left for the airport early the next morning, off my antidepressants for good, but with all the same distractions and doubts I had come with, all the old glitches intact.

13

Los Angeles in the rain. Rain for days. Biblical rain, lashing the boulevards with deep pools of water. Cars creep along cautiously, but still splash the few pedestrians waiting to cross on the curb. By the third day, the sunshine city has passed into deep torpor. I'm on the sofa in our sublet, living out of a suitcase, reading about Simone Weil, of all people. No life could seem more distant, more incomprehensible, from my current vantage point, somewhere in West Hollywood. And yet, I am reading her essays, her journals, the biographies written about her, searching for scraps, for clues. I'm scouring these pages because of a single sentence she once wrote: "Attention is the rarest and purest form of generosity." That line, recorded more than half a century before, had been with me for years. It was indelible. With one sentence, Weil elevated attention outside of the self, raising the stakes to nothing less than how we treat each other.

But I do want to mention one more thing belonging to the difficult year of 2018. As strange and disconcerting as the endless days of rain felt, just one month before, we had passed a much more surreal weekend. That was the weekend when Malibu burned in the Woolsey Fire, one of the worst in the history of the area. In West Hollywood, we were thirty miles from the flames, but by Saturday afternoon, day two of the fire's uncontained progression, the sky turned a color I had never seen before: best described as burnt sienna, the sun blazing ominously from behind gauzy layers of orange brown. As evacuees came down from the canyons, waiting for word on whether their homes would be spared, Josh and I crept tentatively out of the apartment we were staying in. We had an incongruous mission that day: we had to buy wedding rings. Unsure of how or if to proceed, we stopped to get paper face masks at the drugstore. I wanted to cover my nose and mouth. So attired, we drifted with the crowds toward the Grove, the pristine outdoor mall behind the farmers' market. It was right about when we arrived that white ash began falling from the sky. I had the thought that this was the closest I was likely to get to seeing snow in Los Angeles. Josh and I watched the shoppers and pedestrians continue their happy rounds, as if oblivious to the ash falling into their hair.

These are the details of our time and place; this is the era to which we belong. We take to Instagram and Twitter with outrage and righteousness; we ban plastic straws and attempt to shame beef eaters. And we continue with our lives: We buy wedding rings. We conceive babies. It's the attentional paradox of all time: we continue to believe in the future, even while we know what we know. Our world is burning.

What do you do with the truth that you see? What action does attention require? No one I had come across in all my attention research had such a clear reply to this as Simone Weil did. It is all over her short life story, embedded in every biographical detail: Weil believed it was necessary to give absolutely everything.

Weil, once you know about her, has a way of endearing herself, of seducing, through the sheer force of her words. In life, she was intense, single-minded. She provoked extreme loyalty in her friends, family, and students; she cut people out who didn't rise to her standards. I struggle with her character, puzzle over it, chafe against her extremes. But her writing reverberates through the years, shimmering with infinite meaning.

She was born a doctor's daughter, a privileged Jewish girl in Paris. By the end of her short life, she'd be, at different times, a self-described Bolshevik, factory worker, philosopher, mystic, and Christian, yet one who never joined the Church, was never baptized, and admired and learned from the East. Weil abhorred wealth and was repelled by sex and physical touch. She was chaste her entire life. It was Albert Camus who called her "the only great spirit of our times."

Weil was brilliant, flying through her education years ahead of schedule. She was lucky to be born to a family who embraced and enabled her intellect. Her older brother André, who would later become a famous mathematician, taught her everything he learned. Her parents, and especially her mother, Selma, were their daughter's fierce champions, even as Simone's oddities became more and more pronounced. They did not prevent her from acting on her convictions. Simone wore potato sack–inspired ensembles, often stained with ink; her choice of clothing came from her deep sympathy with the working class. Her biographer the late Francine du Plessix Gray described how, at the age of eleven, Simone went missing one afternoon, only to be discovered a few boulevards away, marching with an unemployed workers' protest movement. From a young age, Weil was acutely aware of the inequalities built into her own society and the suffering that resulted. At her own insistence, she spent a summer of her adolescence performing hard manual labor on a fishing boat. A bespectacled, bookish teenager, Simone was not to be denied. This was all the more incongruous because of her physical delicacy: Weil could rarely bring herself to eat more than a few mouthfuls of food and was, throughout her entire life, alarmingly thin.

Weil, like Wallace, like Huxley and William James too, believed in the unsurpassed power of attention. She returned to it again and again in her thoughts, in her writing, and, especially, in her life as an activist. She believed that paying attention could never be a wasted effort. "If we concentrate our attention on trying to solve a problem of geometry, and if at the end of an hour we are no nearer to doing so than at the beginning, we have nevertheless been making progress each minute of that hour in another more mysterious dimension," she writes. "We may not have solved the geometry problem, but our attention itself, the very effort of it, pays off.

"Perhaps he who made the unsuccessful effort will one day be able to grasp the beauty of a line of Racine more vividly on account of it," for example. "Every time that a human being succeeds in making an effort of attention with the sole idea of increasing his grasp of truth, he acquires a greater aptitude for grasping it, even if his effort produces no visible fruit."

In this essay, Weil was writing from her experience in the schoolroom. She had taught in several outposts, all of them far away from Paris, as was traditional for graduates of the elite École normale supérieure. So it was from her vantage as teacher that she wrote: "Most often attention is confused with a muscular effort. If one says to one's pupils: 'Now you must pay attention,' one sees them contracting their brows, holding their breath, stiffening their muscles." But in fact, Weil concludes, this is entirely beside the point, even counter to it. "They have been concentrating on nothing. They have not been paying attention. They have been contracting their muscles."

What they're missing in the flexing of muscles are attention's essential ingredients: Joy. Curiosity. "The intelligence can only be led by desire," she writes. She is describing the ideal classroom, the ideal method of instruction, but by the end of this short essay, "Reflections on the Right Use of School Studies with a View to the Love of God," she has left the classroom behind. She is addressing herself to attention on a cosmic scale when she writes, "The love of our neighbor in all its fullness simply means being able to say to him, 'What are you going through?'" She believes that "only he who is capable of attention can do this."

What are you going through? It's a simple question, but I find it to be one of the most moving lines anywhere in Weil's many volumes of writing.

It was in the pursuit of such attentiveness, such desire to directly understand the experience of others, that Weil was forever rejecting what could have been a comfortable, upper-middle-class life. At twenty-five, frail and afflicted by agonizing headaches, she decided to spend a year working hard labor in various factory jobs in Paris. She believed she had to directly understand what the working class experienced to ever write or say anything valid on the subject. Her time on the factory floor changed her. For the rest of her life, she said, when someone spoke to her "without brutality," she assumed it was by mistake.

But she was closer to answering her eternal question: *What are you going through?*

She was a citizen of her age, entirely, active, observing. In 1932, just twenty-three years old, she had gone to Berlin to see how the Communist Party was faring in Germany. What she saw, with incredible prescience, was Hitler's unimpeded path to power. She came home and published an article predicting the rise of Nazis. A year later, it had come true. When the Spanish Civil War broke out, she quickly left for the front, to fight the fascists (a bad foot injury there likely saved her life).

Weil's perceptions are profound even now, but the facts of her life can be mystifying, even alienating. At every turn, she seems to go too far: the self-starvation, the avoidance of sex and disgust with all physicality, the constant courting of death in her work as an activist. And then, in her twenties, a new twist: her religious conversion. She was sitting in the Solesmes Abbey, just before Easter, 1938, suffering from a bad migraine. But "by an extreme effort of concentration I was able to rise above this wretched flesh," she writes in "Spiritual Autobiography," "to leave it to suffer by itself, heaped up in a corner, and to find a pure and perfect joy in the unimaginable beauty of the chanting and the words." Christ inhabited her soul that day, she would later say.

This, for a hopelessly secular, iPhone-owning city dweller like me is very hard to process, very hard to identify with. I don't know what to do with it. My entire education and culture bias me against such a turn of events. But strangely, if I look closely at my own reaction, I can see that I'm the tiniest bit jealous: jealous of the capacity to believe as Weil believed.

As World War II raged and Hitler closed in, Weil wrote and read furiously. She had fled from Paris to Marseille with her parents, and this is where they stayed, the three Weils in limbo, awaiting visas that would grant them escape from Nazi-occupied France. In these strained, uncertain circumstances, Weil wrote such things in her notebook as: "We have to try to cure our faults by attention and not by will." For Weil, attention was the all-powerful act. She had, of course, radically raised the attention standard, taken the mandate of "paying attention" to a new extreme. "There should not be the slightest discrepancy between one's thoughts and one's way of life," Weil wrote. It is this sentence that perhaps best summarizes her time on this earth. And this is the thing about studying Weil. One must ask oneself, whether one wants to or not: What counts? What is enough?

Weil has inspired many of her readers to action. Susan Sontag, for example, passionately admired Weil, writing in *The New York Review of Books* that Weil was "the person who is excruciatingly identical with her ideas, the person who is rightly regarded as one of the most uncompromising and troubling witnesses to the modern travail of the spirit." In some real sense, Sontag seemed to model herself on Weil: on her intensity, her uncompromising essays, her activism. Was she thinking of Weil when, a few months before her death, she walked onto a stage in South Africa and told the crowd that all writers must "pay attention to the world"?

Yet Sontag also conceded that for almost all of Weil's readers, it would be neither possible nor necessary to copy her extremity, to follow her to all of the uncomfortable places she went. "No one who loves life would wish to imitate her dedication to martyrdom nor would wish it for his children nor for anyone else whom he loves," Sontag continued in her essay. Rather, Sontag believed that "we read writers of such scathing originality for their personal authority, for the example of their seriousness, for their manifest willingness to sacrifice themselves for their truths, and—only piecemeal—for their 'views.'"

Stranded in Marseille, Weil ate less and less. She cited the deprivations of the French soldiers as moral justification for her own eating disorder. Her behavior was growing ever more extreme. She now refused to sleep in beds, or with heat, choosing instead to freeze on the floor. Why should she have comfort when the soldiers did not?

When the Weils' visas came through, Simone sailed with her parents for New York. She knew they wouldn't leave Europe without her and that, as Jews, remaining in France would threaten their lives. In New York, the Weils took an apartment on Riverside Drive, near Columbia. But after a few months, Simone couldn't stand it. She had to return to Europe, to fight with the resistance. As she left for what they all knew might be the last time, she told her stricken parents: "If I had several lives, I would have devoted one of them to you, but I have only one life."

Throughout her final months, she wrote to her parents from England. She was sick and getting sicker, but she never let on how bad her health was, writing letters full of bravado, so that they did not suspect, did not rush to catch a ship as they might otherwise have done, even in wartime. I am already older than Weil was when she died. She lived to be thirty-four, passing away in an English sanitarium from tuberculosis. The only available cure for it was to eat and sleep, but Weil, in her hospital bed, refused to consume any more than what she believed the French soldiers were given on the front lines of the war. To the end, she lived her convictions. Indeed: they killed her.

So what are we to do with a story like Weil's? Are we to follow her lead and walk the plank, sacrificing ourselves so entirely to the world, to the problems and catastrophes of our own age? The true act of paying attention, Weil argued in "Reflections," was one of self-sacrifice, self-erasure. "The soul empties itself of all its own contents in order to receive into itself the being it is looking at, just as he is, in all his truth." I have to admit that I am not prepared to do anything like this. That often, when reading accounts about Weil, I am left cold and sad. I am much more in the Huxley camp. *It is never enough. Never enough. Never enough of beauty. Never enough of love. Never enough of life.*

But still, Weil's words echo in my mind.

I have a theory that we choose the people we write about, out of a vast sea of possibilities, because we find points of identification with them, and that those commonalities, however small, confirm our earliest hunches and spur us on. All through my research, I discovered synchronous biographical overlaps or shared obsessions or both with all of them, all of my attention-minded writers and thinkers, my attention touchstones.

David Foster Wallace was the most obvious. He bridged the gap between attention and addiction; his worries over modern technology mirrored my own. The more I read him, the closer he became. I could shut my eyes and see and hear and smell the bright yellow ball leaving his racket on the tennis courts at Amherst. After all, he was a citizen of the same historical age that I belong to, so that I was alive, hurrying across Union Square on a beautiful bright September day in New York when I got the news that he was dead. It arrived via text message from my friend Dave, the same Dave who had taken me to the emergency room in a New England snowstorm when I was twenty-one, overdosing on Adderall. When I got that text message, I didn't know David Foster Wallace's work yet, not really, but I was stunned, and somehow gutted, and I had to sit down on a bench for a minute or two, catch my breath, as the downtown bustle continued around me.

But it has also been true for those not remotely of my historical moment as well, such as William James, who had lived part of his childhood in Manhattan, a few blocks away from Union Square, in fact, who wanted to define himself out from under his father's sense of who he should be. Huxley, like James, had a family legacy he was always aware of, even burdened by. Perhaps it was partly this line of inheritance that caused him to immigrate to the American West Coast, leaving England and all that was bound up with it, to arrive at the exact same corner of North Kings Road where my brother would, six decades later, take up residence. And, of course, Simone Weil, a Jewish girl born in a vibrant cultural capital with a fiercely tight bond to her mother, Selma Weil, a powerful woman with a clear vision of how things could be, of what could be possible. A mother who reminded me so much of my own.

Weil had inherited a long tradition of a particular kind of attention. In her deepest, most instinctual self, she embodied what had long been seen as attention's highest function: to concentrate on God. And, actually, what occurred to me rather late in the day, only after I'd mostly finished my research, after I'd already lived awhile with Wallace, James, Huxley, and Weil in my head, was this: all four of them were irretrievably drawn to the question of belief. Huxley, directly descended from the man who invented the term "agnostic," nevertheless circled religion for years, experimenting with Vedantic Hinduism, devoting his brilliance to writing *The Perennial Philosophy,* searching for the commonalities among different religions. William James's most abiding masterpiece to date being, of course, *The Varieties of Religious Experience.* Even Wallace, who might seem the least likely candidate, had in fact tried to join the Catholic Church, at least once, and addressed the question of belief in multiple ways.

I wondered about what the connection might be, the dual fascination: how to attend and how to believe. The poet Mary

Oliver died just as I was buried in all things Simone Weil, pondering her legacy. One of Oliver's great themes, of course, was paying attention: to the natural world in particular. In the days after her death, I read through the outpouring of tributes to Oliver's life and work going up online, noting how much her emphasis on attention itself seemed to matter to people, to move them.

For its modesty, its everyday detail, I loved her poem "Praying":

> *It doesn't have to be*
> *the blue iris, it could be*
> *weeds in a vacant lot, or a few*
> *small stones; just*
> *pay attention, then patch*
>
> *a few words together and don't try*
> *to make them elaborate, this isn't*
> *a contest but the doorway*
>
> *into thanks, and a silence in which*
> *another voice may speak.*

It makes perfect sense, then, that it was Oliver who wrote "attention is the beginning of devotion." It's as simple as that, maybe. I think again of the eighteenth-century naturalists, staring all day at their aphids and bees. Eventually, the very force of their attention elevated those tiny insects to beloved, even sacred, objects. Through the power and consistency of their own attention, they fell in love with their bugs.

There was this to consider, as well: "Attention, taken to its highest degree, is the same thing as prayer. It presupposes faith and love." Weil wrote that. I often think about what she meant. To pay attention is to believe there is something worth paying attention to. Even if you don't yet know of what it consists. Even if it hasn't been preselected by an algorithm to play to your interests. Even if it might hurt or disappoint you, scandalize you with its sensibility, or defy you entirely.

Still, blindly, you devote yourself.

When I think of moments of pure attention, one memory often comes back to me: sitting cross-legged on a red leather booth in an Italian restaurant at midnight. This was Brooklyn, late in the winter, not so long ago. Steamy windows against a freezing black night. I was busy asking Josh, my soon-to-be boy-friend, a thousand questions about his childhood, devouring his every reply. This despite being at similar tables, at similar res-taurants many times before, with different men, with whom it hadn't worked out. Sometimes quite painfully so. Nevertheless, we do this, don't we? Manage to find new hope, new capacities for curiosity? That night, my attention was effortless. Entire. This was love, the beginning of love. He is my husband now.

14

Attention can be heartbreaking. You can look up from your dinner, as I recently did, and notice the old man alone in the corner of the busy restaurant, finishing his beer, his eyes ravenously scanning the room, the couples and friends at their tables. His loneliness is palpable, etched into his very expression. It is there for anyone paying attention to see. Now that I've seen it, I can't stop looking. He seeks the crowded room, but he does not belong to it. He pays his bill and makes his exit. I ask the waitress, "Does the man who sat in the corner come here often?" Yes, she tells me. "Does he ever come with someone else?" "Hmm," she says. "Let me think." She asks another waiter and returns to our table. "He always comes alone." That I paid attention to him does not change his life or better it in any way. But I think that it does change mine.

There's another older man at play, of course, or I suppose he'd be called old, though it's difficult to say so. My father, age eighty, sitting in his apartment, without much to look forward to, without a sense of future, as far as he can see. "I don't have a job, darling. I don't have a job." This is his constant refrain now. I don't know what to do with it, how to make conversation with it, how to cure it. It is in fact not entirely true: he broadcasts on the weekends, on his own streaming channel, from a remarkably small amount of equipment set up on his dining room table. He sees himself as a guardian of the American Songbook, communing on the air with his old friends Ella and Frank and all the rest of them, every Saturday and Sunday. He still has his airwaves, but fewer of them. It's a poignant parallel to how he began: as a child, on a homemade radio he could use to broadcast to the neighbors in his apartment building.

He tells me he knows someone his age has to get off the stage. To make room for the young. Meanwhile his wife, who is seven years older, at the tail end of her eighties, is running out the door to paint, to exercise, to go to the Met, casually quoting Plato and Tolstoy on her way. Most days, my father stays inside and reads, or meets friends for lunch. I wonder why he can't seek out the world, as his wife does. But, of course, it's much easier to feel a sense of frustration with my father than it is to acknowledge the full scope of his deep sadness, and therefore my own. The searing empathy we have for our kin. It is hard for me to bear in mind, as I go about my life, how my father now feels about his own.

If we paid attention to everything, all the time, we'd be in hell. Is this why it is so hard to keep our gaze on the ravages of climate change? Why we're able to sit out sipping wine at sidewalk cafés, even as we know the polar bears are starving, the ice sheets collapsing? Even as we know that we will, eventually, die?

The psychoanalyst Harry Stack Sullivan had a term for all this: "selective inattention." It's what we do to keep the pain and anxiety at bay. We learn to do it in infancy, and we keep on doing it for the rest of our life. We cannot always afford to notice.

Meanwhile, I have roamed the world in search of attention, booking passage on trains and planes, then wishing I hadn't, arriving at my destination only to fantasize about my departure. My behavior, it must be said, often looked more like that of a person in search of distraction. I could have continued the search indefinitely. Attention, after all, is the ultimate elusive subject, forever swelling its perimeters. I began to see attention everywhere, as the central fact of so many lives and situations. It became a code word, marking like-minded sensibilities: those who walked around "paying attention to attention," as Huxley's Islanders recommend, as a cure for pain. I looked for these people everywhere, searched the books they left behind for clues.

Everything is potentially relevant. Should I, for example, mention the Rembrandt that stopped me short at the Met Breuer a few years ago? It was an unfinished portrait of St. Bartholomew, holding the knife by which he'd later be flayed. Rembrandt was in the last decade of his life when he painted it. The Met Breuer said it was unfinished, but by the time he painted it, Rembrandt no longer believed that such things as background detail mattered. It was only the essence of things that captured him now. The face, the eyes, the knife. All else fades to brown.

Or maybe Rembrandt's shifting attention is a diversion, a distraction, from the question in front of me now. If I really ask myself, on that most bedrock level of truth, when and how attention became a hallowed force in my life, inevitably I have to admit: it goes back to my mother.

I think of us as we were in February 2015, boarding a train in India, she and I. It was no ordinary train: this one was newly refurbished, redone to look like one of the private trains the Maharajas rode around in, decades before, traveling the country in splendor. Or so it was advertised. It was to be a seven-day train ride, taking a circuitous, tourist's route from Mumbai to Goa, stopping each morning at a different destination along the way.

My mother, intrepid investigative journalist that she is, had gotten an assignment to write about this train ride for a travel magazine. And she was desperate, she told me, to see the Ellora Caves, the legendarily beautiful UNESCO World Heritage Site, intricately carved out of a cliff, still almost entirely preserved. The caves are not easy to get to, located in a part of India we wouldn't otherwise be likely to visit. All the more reason to remain on this train, then, which would arrive at the caves around day five of its meandering itinerary.

My mother: a journalist with a vibrant career, insatiable for more experience, more intrigue, more life, more Ellora. Me: an insecure thirty-two-year-old, wondering how I found myself painfully single, waiting for my first book to be published, anxious about my future, and about to be stuck on a train in remotest India with my mother for a week. So there we were, boarding the train to great pomp and circumstance, Indian musicians in bright shades of pinks and oranges gathered on the platform, seeing us off with utmost fanfare.

Once aboard, I couldn't help but notice the train didn't seem to live up exactly to Maharaja standards. But there *was* a treadmill, a strange thing to contemplate doing as the Indian countryside whipped by outside the window. There were also private cabins, which was cheering, until we discovered that because of the uneven train tracks, one spent the night bouncing up and down upon one's mattress.

Each morning, my mother and I gathered bleary-eyed in the breakfast car and laid out a map on the table in front of us, sketching out a possible escape route, should we decide that we simply had to get off the train that very day. By which provincial airport would we flee? But every single morning, after completing that daily thought experiment, my mother turned to me. "If we leave now," she would say, "we won't get to see the Ellora Caves."

And so, we stayed.

On the fourth day of this experience, at around 4:30 in the morning, a loud knock came on each cabin door. The train was stopped; all was inky darkness outside the windows. Today's activity was tiger spotting at a private tiger preserve. The catch: tigers, threatened with extinction, were not known to be commonplace in this part of India.

We were all roused from our beds and driven through the chilly darkness. The preserve we were taken to was owned by a father and son; the son in his mid-thirties, educated in the West, his father sixty-something, less in touch with Americanness in all its forms. Perhaps because my mother was there as the American journalist, it was the son who personally drove the two of us around in a bumpy open-aired jeep for the next three hours, in an attempt to spot a tiger. As we proceeded over the rough dirt, in the freezing morning, I felt myself shrink into the ungrateful teenage version of my own psychology, unable in that moment to feel the extraordinary privilege of just being there. I wrapped my scarf tight around my body and glared out at our tiger-free surroundings. Occasionally, the owner/driver would stop the jeep and point to an ambiguous pawprint in the dirt. If only we'd been here an hour earlier, he would say. My mother and I fell to silence.

Finally, the son brought us to the small house where we would be spending the next eight hours with the rest of the train's passengers: a single room, with no air-conditioning, under the fierce Indian sun. This is where we would sit and wait, we were told, until it was time for the second tiger-spotting attempt, at dusk.

I told my mother I was going to take a nap in a room in the back, before we were swarmed by the train's other passengers, who had all gone off in their own private jeeps, and with whom we were about to spend what was clearly going to be the most pointless day of my life to date. I had left all my reading material on board the train—a fatal error, for which I was now furious at myself. I was exhausted and defeated, steeped in the madness of the day. I could tell that even my mother was at her wit's end: unsmiling, she firmly asked the son to bring out a map and help her figure out by which remote airport or train station we might be able to escape to Mumbai, at once. Patiently, he sat with her, to demonstrate what such a feat would require. First, a six-hour drive to . . .

I retreated to a twin bed. When I woke up, I was still in the middle of nowhere, India, all of that day's pointlessness still lying in wait. I returned to the main room. And there, at the single small table, sat the father, the son, and my mother, who had her notebook open in front of her, her tape recorder running, and was now utterly rapt by the life stories of these two men, asking them a hundred questions, furiously writing down their every reply. She could have been Bernstein and Woodward, for the intensity of her investigation. She had departed the realm of the pointless and was now, I could see, in a state of complete and total reportorial flow, absorbed by her curiosity, her unflagging attention to the experiences of these two men and how they had come to run their tiger preserve. She was, in other words, in her own Place of Deep Absorption. From across the room, though I'd never have admitted it then and do so only reluctantly now, I was in awe.

In fact, it was one of a thousand such occasions, the lesson being the same each time: paying attention takes you outside yourself. Paying attention can turn any situation, however pointless, however painful, into sheer human richness. Even through the hell of watching my father's career end as it did, the same truth applied.

"Take notes," my mother told me.

There's another thread here, though, I think worth pointing out, because I believe it's something of a universal. Attention is the value we aspire to but also what we castigate ourselves with, punishing ourselves for our own imperfections, our own fail-ures to concentrate. In India, I was in awe of my mother, but I was also angry with myself, for failing to be a good traveler, absorbing the world around me without a trace of complaint. It is exactly this view, of my own attentional shortcomings, that had gotten me in trouble when I was eighteen years old, convinced me that my brain needed attention pills in order to be good enough, a conviction I couldn't shake for more than a decade, and even then, not entirely. It's a suspicion that haunts me now, still, all these years later. It's a question I still haven't answered.

Meanwhile, I have yet to enroll in a digital detox, replace my iPhone with an old-school flip phone, or even get off Instagram.

I have few concrete suggestions for reining in screen time, no helpful digital minimalism strategies to offer. Yet the very experience of thinking about attention—of its history, its ambiguity, and its power—has been transformative. It has changed me.

It's the simplest act, really. To look up, as often as I can. To behold the world, as it is, right now, all around me.

Epilogue to the Vintage Books Edition (2021)

On Christmas Eve 2019, I lay, paralyzed by an epidural, in a bed in the labor and delivery ward of Mount Sinai Hospital. For hours, as my body experienced contractions that I couldn't feel, I stared out the second-floor window onto the treetops of Central Park, directly across the street. As the contractions continued and the morning blurred into afternoon, my mother and brother came to the park and stood in the field directly opposite the hospital. Josh, at the window, was the only one who could see them. But their presence there was as obscurely comforting as the familiar treetops. I bring this up because three short months after that afternoon, white medical tents would be erected exactly where my mother and brother stood waving, waiting for the baby. The tents were brought in to receive the overflow of Covid-19 patients, or perhaps the overflow of bodies. I never was clear on exactly their purpose, only what they signified: New York was now the center of the center of the storm, as close to the edge of its capacities as it had ever been. The sight of the white tents, like something out of a Civil War movie, was one more shock in a season of shock, in a city that was, by that spring, on its knees.

This is what we all know, because we all lived through it: the retreat inside, the terror of crowds, of surfaces, of public life in each and every one of its manifestations. When we did go out, we went like bandits. Friends took their children to play in the cemetery instead of the park. The rest of the time, we lived on-screen. All my purist intentions to limit the baby's exposure to screens (I would have none of it, I had righteously announced while pregnant) went up like secondhand smoke, the kind I steered his stroller into the street in order to avoid. But there was no longer any hope of getting him away from screens. During Zoom meetings, there was no place for him to go except my lap; there was no way for him to see his grandparents except via FaceTime.

I read that Eric Schmidt, the former CEO of Google, said in an interview that he hoped the pandemic would make us all just "a little bit grateful" for Big Tech. "The benefit of these corporations—which we love to malign—in terms of the ability to communicate . . . the ability to get information, is profound—and I hope people will remember that when this thing is finally over," he said in a livestream to the Economic Club of New York.

And of course, we *were* at least a little bit grateful. Weren't we? It often felt to me like the pandemic confirmed tech's total ascendancy in our lives; as if, eerily enough, the technology had been invented to provide for this very moment. We were now all citizens of a virtual landscape we couldn't escape. There was nowhere to go that was as safe as these sterile, bodiless exchanges.

Our time on-screen shot up ever higher. We've all lived through it, yet the numbers still astound. Consider this: By September 2020, average daily online "content consumption" had doubled since the start of the pandemic, from three hours and seventeen minutes to six hours and fifty-nine minutes, according to a study done by DoubleVerify. (They included ten thousand consumers from five different countries, including the United States.) And children's screen-time habits, of course, were dramatically upended. Now most American kids went to school online, or partially online, in addition to everything else they already did online. By only the third month of quarantine, children ages four to fifteen in the United States were online for double the amount of time they had been in the same period the year before. A study published in a journal of ophthalmology found that, over the course of 2020, rates of myopia in 120,000 Chinese children increased by more than three times what they'd been for the previous five years. These children, by the way, were between the ages of six and eight. The story emerging from these statistics and so many others like them confirms what we know. If we could, if we were fortunate enough to have the choice, we left behind the physical world.

Besides safety, besides routine, what was so notably lost in that viral spring of 2020 was the sensory. The neighbor's bounding dog we didn't dare pet. The dear friend we couldn't embrace when we came upon him on the street. The smile we couldn't see behind its spooky mask. All of these moments registered in the body like micro tragedies—and they added up. We had our phones and our computers and our televisions, but they did not dispel the boredom and loneliness and grief.

As the weeks went by, our apartment grew messier and messier, until it had officially passed the boundary of what could be dealt with. Alone now to care for our baby, barely sleeping, trying to work, we somehow couldn't muster the energy or time to even change our sheets. It was like that. Impossible. Whenever I could, I did a pass with the vacuum cleaner, using the nozzle not only to collect dust but to shove piles of clutter back against the apartment's too-tight walls. It seemed that everyone we knew took to Instagram to display their stunning talent for cooking dinner. But at our apartment, I was flinging hamburger meat into a pan and eating raw cookie dough from the deli.

The deli was our beacon. The deli would ever so occasionally get shipments of tiny bottles of Purell, and when it did I would text friends in the neighborhood: "It's in." The man behind the counter would sell only four to a customer, and he did so at an exorbitant markup. The Purell he hawked came in Christmas flavors, like Warm Holiday Treats, a tiny irony in a season of terror. A year later, I think of those little Purell bottles as the locus of so much magical thinking, as if they contained some mythical antidote to a dangerous poison, as if they could protect us from the particles of virus swarming the air in our city.

Through these stunned, silent spring days, attention was constantly on my mind. Of course, there were more immediate concerns: Would there be a hospital bed? Would there be a ventilator? But after years of thinking about attention, I was acutely aware of my own. I thought of Mihaly Csikszentmihalyi. I wanted to find his sublimation, his divine flow, the way he escaped from the bombs falling on Budapest by staring at his chessboard. I didn't want to miss my son's precious babyhood because I was staring at my phone in fear. In the afternoons, when the loneliness threatened to overwhelm me and I had already called everyone I could call, I pushed the baby around in his stroller, playing what I thought of as my attention game. There were almost no cars then in our Brooklyn neighborhood, just silence punctuated by the wail of ambulances. People freely walked in the streets, if they walked outside at all. I was on a hunt every day to collect surreal details, images that captured this impossible moment in time. I wrote them all down: the tables still perfectly set for dinner at the Greek restaurant on the corner, the silverware gleaming even as dust began to gather on the floor. The line that stretched three blocks long outside the famous food co-op, like a Soviet breadline, so long that people had taken to bringing chairs to sit in while they waited. The jazz that still played at the fancy food store while terrified shoppers raced by the expensive cheeses, grabbing staples and returning to shelter in place. The possum, sensing the sudden scarcity of humans, that dared to run up and down the neighbor's stoop with its long hairless tail waving in the air like a primitive antenna.

I wanted to be able to tell my baby son about these details one day, but the very act of collecting them, I noticed, did something for my mood. It had to do with the deliberate flexing of attention: I reclaimed myself in those moments. Out on the streets, gathering details, I was no longer the stressed-out lump on the sofa, passively consuming information. Purposefully directing my attention gave me agency again.

A constant refrain that spring was "I can't read. I can't focus." It became sort of fashionable to admit one was too scattered to think. I began calling experts to make sense of it. Or maybe it was an excuse to have more people to call: I hungered for the human voice on the other end of the line.

I called Adam Gazzaley, a neuroscientist who studies attention at the University of California, San Francisco. I found him sheltering in place in the Mission District, with an already detailed plan he had devised to protect his own focus. It's not that stress is inherently bad for attention, he told me. In fact, we have better attention when we are a little bit stressed compared to when we are completely relaxed. It's too much stress, and for too long, that threatens to shatter and scatter us. To this end, he had designed an intricate schedule for himself and sent it out to every member of his lab at UCSF, advising them to get out of bed every day, to get dressed. To exercise. (Gazzaley had two daily workouts written on his schedule, one in the morning, one in the afternoon.) To not consume news all day. (He also had allotted two appointments with the news.) At week five of the quarantine, he was organized and galvanized, and I envied him that.

"This is not just a crisis of our respiratory systems or even of our economics; this is a crisis of our minds," he told me. "Attention is part of the mental health framework—in fact it's the foundation of the pyramid. If your attention is impaired, all of it is vulnerable. You can't regulate your emotional content, so then you have mood problems. You can't focus on your significant other; now you have relationship problems. You can't focus on work; now you have productivity at work problems. It is the basis of how we interact with the world. So when attention becomes fragmented and overwhelmed, it cascades through everything."

As we spoke, I pictured him in his gleaming Mission District apartment, preparing to Peloton or to stand on his head or whatever insider trick neuroscientists use to optimize their brain state. Meanwhile, directly on the other side of my laptop screen lay a jumble of diapers and onesies and other newborn accoutrements. My desk had somehow morphed into my baby's changing table. Gazzaley's routine for self-preservation was as inaccessible to me in the spring of 2020 as a flight to Europe.

Just before we hung up, Gazzaley started talking about the "chronic stress" implications of Covid-19. I listened but couldn't quite accept what he was getting at. It was April 2020, and I was still thinking in two-week units. Maybe monthlong units. By August, by the fall, things would be different, wouldn't they? I couldn't then conceive of "chronic." Of a year going by. Perhaps longer. "Right now everyone just wants to get through the day, it's a need to survive, but we don't really understand the implications of all the screen time," he told me. "We're doing a big uncontrolled experiment right now. Especially with children."

I called Sherry Turkle, the psychologist, author, and MIT professor who has spent much of her career documenting our evolving relationship with technology. Turkle had expressed deep ambivalence in her recent books about our growing screen time, chronicling what she perceives as a decline in empathy, connected to the decline in face-to-face interactions. I expected that she would be alarmed now by our "big uncontrolled experiment." But in fact, that wasn't her thinking at all. I found Turkle hiding from the virus in Provincetown, by the beach, the same beach the naturalist and philosopher Henry David Thoreau had once walked, all thirty miles up Cape Cod.

On her computer, she was watching Yo-Yo Ma play his cello every day from his study. She was watching Patrick Stewart recite Shakespearean sonnets from his porch. And like most of us, she was reflecting on the ways in which our screens were saving us. "We've received the equivalent of pornography, of political pornography," she said, her outrage toward the government's handling of the pandemic palpable. "We've been lied to. We've been told to relax just at the point when we should have quarantined. We have been told the opposite of the truth, and we have had to go to our screens to try and figure out more truthful actors. So in a way we've used our screens for detective work. Were it not for our screens, we would be in a much worse state."

I knew of course that Turkle was right, yet I was still unsure how to balance arming myself with information and being swallowed whole by it. I mentioned to Turkle how much I yearned to channel the transcendent focus of a Mihaly Csikszentmihalyi. To use this time for some kind of higher purpose. "Right now, that's aspirational," she said. Just as I had fought against Adam Gazzaley's invoking of the chronic, of the idea that this was our new *life*, I also didn't wish to accept Turkle's prognosis. I wanted to somehow access a reserve of focus, to rewrite the story of 2020, to preserve what I could of my own mind, without knowing then exactly what that could even mean.

Almost a full year later, I called Turkle again. In New York, we were coming up on the end of a long, tough winter. So much had come true from Adam Gazzaley's predictions about our collective mental health. Everything bad had soared: rates of depression, addiction, loneliness. But as well, there was, for the first time in a long time, real hope. A presidency had ended; vaccines had arrived.

Turkle was still in Provincetown, still looking out at Thoreau's beach. So it was almost inevitable that he should come up. "Thoreau's whole thing wasn't about being alone," she told me. "It was about living *deliberately*." And that was the opportunity Turkle believed we had before us: to consciously decide, now that the rules had all been rewritten by the extraordinary year we'd survived, what we wanted to return to, and what we didn't. We didn't even need a trip to Walden Pond like Thoreau. The pandemic had made it clear that no single aspect of our life as we'd known it was, in fact, inevitable.

As I write this, we are poised on the edge of a new chapter. Everywhere I go, people are talking about vaccines. They are talking about the return to normal life, whatever that might mean. I think about Turkle's words, and Thoreau's before her, often: what it would look like to live more deliberately, even though our technology isn't going anywhere. When I type Thoreau's famous line—"I went to the woods because I wished to live deliberately"—into Google, I'm directed to a website to read the full passage. And there, right next to Thoreau's impassioned cry "to front only the essential facts of life, and see if I could not learn what it had to teach, and not, when I came to die, discover that I had not lived," an advertisement for a used purple Prada purse throbs on the screen, blinking to achieve maximal conspicuousness. The ad successfully nullifies the effect of Thoreau's magisterial words, sucking the power from his timeless text, which I have to strain to read. This is the framework we have, the framework we're in: distraction on distraction. So what do we do? How do we take back our minds?

These aren't simple questions to answer, if you're not prepared to head for the woods. But for me, deliberateness starts with an awareness of something I've always on some level known, but lived in a new way over the last year. Attention doesn't have to be perfect. In fact, it never is, and it never has been. But it's *ours*, to pay as we choose. And therein lies its power—and its preciousness.

April 2021

Acknowledgments

It is hard to put words to the gratitude I feel for my editor, Dan Frank. His assistant, Vanessa Haughton, put much thought and talent into making these sentences better. Thank you to them both and to the whole Pantheon team.

Thank you to my agent, Elyse Cheney, and to Alex Jacobs, for his elevating input in the early stages. Ilena Silverman edited an earlier version of the Adderall chapters for *The New York Times Magazine*. I am deeply grateful for the depth and precision she brought to that piece.

Beatrice Hogan, fact-checker extraordinaire: thank you.

Many thanks to Nick Seaver and his students at Tufts for including me in their stimulating How to Pay Attention class; those conversations have greatly enriched this book.

I have the good fortune to be surrounded by friends whose intelligence and creativity lift me up every single day. For help in ways too innumerable to document, thank you to my beloveds Risa Needleman, Aatish Taseer, Jessica Bennett, and Liese Mayer. Thank you to

Dave Wallace-Wells and Ariel Schulman, who helped me hammer out the idea that would become this book. To Stefan Block, whose astonishing edits went above and beyond the bounds of friendship and to whom I am forever grateful. To Peggy Noonan for stalwart guidance on language and life; to David Sauvage for the deep read at the eleventh hour and for a decade of friendship and attention; to Emily Galvin and Jesse Rissman for their thoughtful input; and to Michael Garfinkle, Grey Gersten, Sara Wilson, Meghan Kennedy, and Rachel Smith for profound conversations they were always willing to have.

Thank you to my dear brother, Adam Schwartz, who is on this journey with me; to my in-laws Adria and Fred; to Sidne, Candy, and Franny too, for the unconditional support; and, of course, to James and Kat, always.

To my own parents, all of them, Ernie, Ellie, Zohra, and Jonathan, and especially to my mother, Marie Brenner, my north star, who took me to see the world.

And last, but mostly, to Josh, who came into my life just as I was beginning to write this book, and changed it completely. Nothing, but nothing, would be the same without you.

ALSO BY

CASEY SCHWARTZ

IN THE MIND FIELDS
Exploring the New Science of Neuropsychoanalysis

Neuroscience and psychoanalysis are historically opposed responses to the age-old quest to understand ourselves—one focused on the brain and the other on the mind. As part of a pioneering program to look for common ground between the two warring disciplines, Casey Schwartz spent one year immersed in psychoanalytic theory at the Anna Freud Centre, and the next year studying the brain among Yale's cutting-edge neuroscientists. She came away with a clear picture of the distance between the two fields: while neuroscience is lacking in attention to lived experience, psychoanalysis is often too ephemeral and subjective. Armed with this awareness, Schwartz set out to study the main pioneers in the emerging and controversial field of neuropsychoanalysis. With passion and humor, she makes a trenchant argument for a hybrid scientific culture that will allow the two approaches to thrive together.

Biography

THE BRAIN
The Story of You
by David Eagleman

Locked in the silence and darkness of your skull, your brain fashions the rich narratives of your reality and your identity. Join renowned neuroscientist David Eagleman for a journey into the questions at the mysterious heart of our existence. What is reality? Who are "you"? How do you make decisions? Why does your brain need other people? How is technology poised to change what it means to be human? In the course of his investigations, Eagleman guides us through the world of extreme sports, criminal justice, facial expressions, genocide, brain surgery, gut feelings, robotics, and the search for immortality. This is the story of how your life shapes your brain, and how your brain shapes your life.

Science

GENDER AND OUR BRAINS
How New Neuroscience Explodes the Myths of the Male and Female Minds
by Gina Rippon

Gina Rippon unpacks the stereotypes that surround us from our earliest moments and shows how these messages mold our ideas of ourselves and even shape our brains. By exploring new, cutting-edge neuroscience, Rippon urges us to move beyond a binary view of the brain and to see instead this complex organ as highly individualized, profoundly adaptable and full of unbounded potential. Rigorous, timely and liberating, *Gender and Our Brains* has huge implications for women and men, for parents and children, and for how we identify ourselves.

Science

Printed in the United States
by Baker & Taylor Publisher Services